100
Ways to
Overcome
Shyness

100

Ways to

Overcome Shyness

Go From Self-Conscious to Self-Confident

Barton Goldsmith, PhD and Marlena Hunter, MA

The Career Press, Inc.
Wayne, NJ

100 WAYS TO OVERCOME SHYNESS
TYPESET BY KRISTIN GOBLE
Cover design by Howard Grossman
Printed in the U.S.A.

To order this title, please call toll-free 1-800-CAREER-1 (NJ and Canada: 201-848-0310) to order using VISA or MasterCard, or for further information on books from Career Press.

CAREER
PRESS

The Career Press, Inc.
12 Parish Drive
Wayne, NJ 07470
www.careerpress.com

Library of Congress Cataloging-in-Publication Data
Goldsmith, Barton.
  100 ways to overcome shyness : go from self-conscious to self-confident / Barton Goldsmith and Marlena Hunter.
    pages cm
  ISBN 978-1-60163-369-9 (paperback) -- ISBN 978-1-60163-383-5 (ebook) 1. Bashfulness. 2. Self-confidence. 3. Interpersonal communication. I. Hunter, Marlene E. (Marlene Elva), 1931- II. Title. III. Title: One hundred ways to overcome shyness.

  BF575.B3G65 2015
  158.2--dc23

                                                           2015010671

To Marlena's lovely children, Kato and Deanna.

Grow together and be there for one another whenever you need a listener, a shoulder to lean on, or someone to share your laughter and tears.

ACKNOWLEDGMENTS

Together we would like to thank Michael Pye, Adam Schwartz, Kirsten Dalley, and everyone else at Career Press for asking us to write this book and for their support in getting it right. Thank you for this wonderful opportunity to make this dream become a reality.

We would also like to thank our clients for sharing their lives with us and allowing us to be a part of their journeys. We offer our heartfelt gratitude to the readers who have chosen this book to help guide them.

Marlena would like to thank all of the colleagues and supervisors who believed in her, with special mention to Dr. Martha Koo, MD, for offering her a wonderful opportunity to be a part of the research team at the Manhattan Beach Professional Group; and to Dr. Mandana Shahoveisi and Dr. Linda Schnaible, for providing her with a unique opportunity to work in the field of psychology in a private practice setting.

Marlena also wishes to thank her entire family, including her mother, Joyce; her brother, Curtis; and her grandparents, aunts, uncles, cousins, nieces, and nephews, as well as her father, Ira, who passed away when she was 11 years old and inspired her to work in the field of psychology. He will always be remembered as a strong man with a positive attitude, full of energy. She would also like to thank her two dearest friends, Talia and Georg. And, finally, to the one and only pet she has ever had—Spencer, whom she still misses.

Barton wishes to acknowledge his mentors, Dr. Harville Hendrix, Dr. Elizabeth Kubler-Ross, Dr. Shawn Shea, and Dr. David Viscott, for the outstanding training and rich friendships. They are all thought of in the brightest of lights. He would also like to recognize his respected colleagues Dr. Brian Satt and Dr. Peggy DuBious. Barton also thanks his friends: Tam, Caila and Cash, Jeb, and Pam, as well as Silva, who will always hold a part of his heart, as will his pets, Mercy and Phoenix. In addition, he would like to thank the readers of his column and previous books. And finally, a shout-out to two great therapists, Linda Metzger and Dr. Linda Loomis, the mothers he never had.

CONTENTS

INTRODUCTION

If you feel that your shyness has held you back and prevented you from living a full life, this book will give you the tools you need to open yourself up to all that you've been missing out on because of the shyness factor.

Most likely you picked up this book because you have felt limited by your shyness and are hoping to find some answers. Fortunately, there are many answers. You are not destined to live a life of quiet desperation on the sidelines because of shyness, social anxiety, generalized anxiety disorder, or even autism. The techniques we share in this book have been designed to help you on many levels. The most important thing to remember is to take things one step at a time. You can't eat the whole pizza at once (unless you want to get sick), and overcoming shyness is no different. It's not just about getting over your fear of rejection; it will go to the very core of how you live your whole life.

Statistics show that people who live solitary lives don't live as long as those who enjoy deep and meaningful connections with family and friends. Each step you take to vanquish the fear that is holding you back will add more years to your life and, perhaps, more life to your years. If you want a more socially active life and want to be able to have conversations with others—even complete strangers—without wanting to run and hide, then this book is for you.

Use this book in the way that makes sense to you. Read it straight through, or skip around and pick topics that jump out at you. Refer back to it often. Almost every chapter has an exercise or actionable suggestions to help you deal with and overcome the pain of shyness. Many different situations are discussed, so you should be able to find something that addresses your particular challenges.

Give yourself the gift of human interaction. It is necessary for a full life and second only to food, safety, and shelter when it comes to our most basic human needs.

1.

Accepting Rejection

Self-esteem has to do with our perception of our own worth. If we have low self-esteem, others will pick up on that; this can put us in a vulnerable position, one in which we aren't valued in the way we desire. If we lack ego-resilience, we are easily hurt. If we don't have the skills to build self-esteem, this can effectively cripple us and prevent us from attaining our life goals. Fact is, we often avoid rejection to protect our egos. Shy people in particular tend to experience rejection more often due to their expectation of being rejected. But sometimes it really is "all in your mind." One artist who wanted to get his work into a particular art gallery was rejected until his two-thousandth application, when he was finally offered the venue of his dreams.

If you have ego-resilience, however, there are actually some benefits to rejection. If you are shy and have recently experienced rejection—let's say you were turned down for a job—try to benefit from it. Use it as a motivator to continue your job search and to find acceptance somewhere else. If you make an effort to build up your ego, you will find that your ego becomes more resilient. You can use hurt and rejection as fuel to persevere and succeed in life.

Nervous habits such as a low tone of voice or being unable to make eye contact with others can send shyness signals to others. When you are speaking, keep your voice clear and strong, and ensure that you are understood by enunciating your words. Shy people sometimes fear that they will seem aggressive or disrespectful if they speak in a loud or strong tone. If you feel this way, don't worry about speaking too loudly. If others are struggling to hear you, they may become frustrated. If you are shy, the last thing you want to hear is someone asking you to repeat yourself.

No matter how much rejection you experience, never give up on our dreams and goals. Use each experience of rejection as motivation to try harder. If you are going through struggles, think of your adversity and let that become your fuel. If you want something badly enough, you won't take rejection personally—or, at least it won't sting as much, because you'll be focused on the goal, not the feeling of being rejected. Learn to accept rejection by not taking it personally. If someone rejects you, use it as motivation instead.

Exercise

Think of an occasion when you were rejected and *did* take it personally. How could you respond differently next time? Think of some healthy ways to respond to rejection and different ways you could use the experience of rejection to grow and learn. Everyone faces rejection at times. If you find yourself thinking negative thoughts often, try using some positive self-talk. Tell yourself not to take it personally, and remember something positive about yourself.

Don't let the fear of rejection make you shy. Use the possibility of rejection as a motivator for being less shy.

2.

Altruistic Love

Altruism has many benefits, the most important of which is the way in which it contributes to the greater good. Some scientists suggest that altruism is nature's way of increasing the odds of survival in a group because it increases the fitness of every member of that group. Shy people are often especially altruistic because they're too shy to ask for anything for themselves. But doing favors for others without expecting anything in return can help us feel good about *ourselves*.

If you want to love and be loved in return, you need to consider whether you may be putting stressors onto others that are actually your own personal problems to deal with. It's important to avoid being selfish. This means not continually dumping your own problems—the issues you're having with a colleague at work, for example—onto your loved ones. Think of altruism as a kind of sacrifice that reduces the burdens on your friends and family members. If you are loving and altruistic, you are more likely to be admired, loved, and respected in return—in part because you won't be overwhelming others with your own needs and issues. In addition, your relationships are more likely to grow and last.

There are several ways you can vent your problems safely if you're going through rough times. These include attending psychotherapy, taking up a new hobby, attending meetups, going out with friends, and going to the gym, among a multitude of other options. If you still feel unheard at times, talking to a therapist can help you process your negative emotions without foisting them onto your love ones. You can also try taking a meditation, yoga, or tai chi class, all of which can relieve stress and help you in your personal life.

If you are shy, you may be deeply afraid to love others because you want to avoid being hurt or disappointed by them in the future. When we love ourselves, we improve ourselves, and others become attracted to our positive qualities. We all want to be happy, and we are all more attracted to happy people. Love comes when we care about someone else's happiness. If you are shy, you may feel embarrassed about being on the receiving end of acts of kindness or altruism. Remind yourself that it is okay to let others show *you* altruistic love.

Exercise

Try being more aware of what others need and the ways in which you can help them, but—and here's the key—*without expecting anything in return.* This is one way to show altruism toward others, and I promise you it will help you build positive relationships with them.

If you practice altruistic love, and are able to set aside shyness and the fear of being hurt, even just temporarily, you will notice that the altruism you are giving out will come back to you in spades—simply because you have set aside your own negative projections.

3.

Anger Can Make You Shy

Deep internal anger at the world or even one person can keep you stuck in your shyness, especially when you use your anger as an excuse not to reach out and heal the problem or get on with your life. At times, I admit I have been mad at the world and some of the people in it, and thus have retreated to the comfort of my solitude. But that gets lonely and boring pretty quickly. I dislike isolation as a constant in my universe, but sometimes my emotions get the best of me, and I sit and stew in my own angry juices. What a waste!

My dad once told me that in a discussion or a relationship, the first one who gets mad, loses. It has proven too true in my life thus far, so I do my best to keep my anger contained (unless I'm with my therapist). It does me no good, and only serves to push other people away and even hurt their feelings—not something I want to do. Instead, I do what I can to focus my energy and creativity on more positive behaviors. It takes some effort and awareness, and you have to catch yourself before you lash out or say something inappropriate (and almost everything said in anger is). Avoid getting stuck in fruitless attempts at retaliation when you get mad at someone. Better to let go of the anger than to waste time and energy doing something snarky to hurt the person who ticked you off. It's just going to distance you further, and usually that is not the best outcome. It helps if you have the presence of mind to say it to yourself first and imagine how the other person would react. If you have goodwill toward that person, you probably won't want to hurt him or her.

Interestingly, anger can work the opposite way, as well, giving you the energy and courage you need to confront someone who angered you—not something that shy people normally do, or do comfortably. Even though you could make an argument that this process results in psychological growth, it's just too toxic to use. Bottom line: Think about it before you give someone a piece of your mind. You may need all you have to deal with this shyness stuff!

No matter how much energy and effort you have invested in a person or project, someone or something is going to make you angry. Fortunately, you always have a choice. Make the right one, the one that allows you to be

who you are and stick to your beliefs without hurting yourself or the relationship. Both are hard to rebuild and virtually impossible to replace.

4.

Anxiety

Anxiety is *the* primary learning problem in psychopa-
thology. Anxiety can be learned in response to any
stimulus. An airplane flight, a dog, even the sound of a
phone ringing can cause anxiety in some people. Shy people can also experience related physiological problems along
with anxiety, as habitual responses to specific stimuli. These
responses might include a tension headache, an upset stomach, sweating, and difficulty sleeping. Most phobias are conditioned anxieties that eventually lead to avoidance. Because
shyness is learned through conditioning, it can be unlearned
through counter-conditioning.

One way to feel more comfortable before and during an
anxiety-inducing event is to do a few simple things to prepare and organize beforehand. For example, you can learn
about the venue so that you won't be over- or under-dressed.
Being dressed inappropriately for an event can weigh on
your mind the entire time you're there, making you uncomfortable and even anxious. Being preoccupied with thoughts

such as *I look like an idiot* or *When will this be over?* will make you want to exit stage left. Knowing what to wear can help you avoid feeling self-conscious during the event. If you need to change clothes, bring your outfit with you during the day and change at the gym or a friend's place after work.

Arriving on time or even a bit early to an event can also help reduce feelings of awkwardness. Think about how you usually feel when you enter a room full of strangers. If you are a new face, it is normal to feel nervous and assume that all eyes are on you, especially if you're late and everyone is already mingling. Try not to look like a deer caught in headlights. Just calmly make your way through each room until you find a comfortable spot or a kind-looking person to talk to. If you are introduced to someone you don't know, ask her how she knows the host/hostess. When you are invited to an event and you decide to go alone, it is often helpful to arrive early. That way, you can get comfortable in the new environment before it becomes busy and intimidating.

Entering a strange place for the first time can be really frightening for someone who is shy. But the longer you are there, the more comfortable you'll become. So why not get an early start? You can even make friends before the event begins by volunteering to help check guests in or set up tables. This way, you become a part of the event and not just a bystander.

Also, pay close attention to your behavioral cues such as eye contact and facial expressions. Do you worry about whether others will notice you? If so, smile. Because we are all conditioned to smile at someone who is smiling at us, someone will almost certainly return the friendly gesture and smile back at you.

Exercise

If you've ever had an anxiety attack during a conversation at a social event, you know how embarrassing and downright scary this can be. You can actually prevent this by being in tune with your breathing. When you notice that you are taking shorter and shallower breaths, do some deep breathing exercises. Breathe in through your nose and out through your mouth, slowly. Imagine that you are in a peaceful place, watching a sunset or the weather, with no agenda beyond just enjoying the moment.

5.

Autism

I once had a client who suffered from extreme shyness, to the point that it interfered with his ability to function professionally and socially. He had been diagnosed as falling on the autism spectrum. Socialization is one of the greatest difficulties for people who are dealing with autism spectrum disorder (ASD). Their behavior is easily mistaken for extreme shyness, rudeness, or even social phobia.

Whether you are simply shy or somewhere on the autism spectrum, you may find it difficult to cope with new challenges and new surroundings. For example, if you're starting out at a new job, unless you are lucky enough to already have some of your friends there, you can face considerable social pressure. Lack of socialization may lead to unhealthy relationships and can increase a person's risk for psychiatric disorders such as depression and anxiety. People with ASD actually long for social interaction and relationships, but their tendency to be loners gets in the way of engagement with others.

Fortunately, engaging in very structured social activities has been shown to yield positive results for people who tend to need reinforcement in order to engage with other people. To find structured activities to take part in, look for a group that can provide the social support you need. Look for activities that are facilitated by social interactions. Socially appropriate behaviors are a necessity in most, if not all, social activities. Attend weekly support-group meetings with new friends to discuss and follow up on your progress. Discussing your activities with your friends is also a good way to become more committed because it will lead to invitations to events and reminders about your activities. Your ultimate goal will be to be able to model social interactions without thinking about it.

If you are extremely shy or you suffer from ASD, you should try joining a structured activity that requires commitment and accountability. Consistency and a balanced schedule can help you become and remain socially active. Stay connected to the other people involved in your activity, and have them follow up with you when you start to feel less engaged or when you are lacking motivation.

Exercise

Invite a friend from an activity you are attending to coffee beforehand or afterward, especially if you are falling behind, and ask him or her for help. Just asking for help opens a dialogue, which is a great exercise for reducing shyness.

The goal is to be able to engage in social activities more or less comfortably on your own. Your shyness will virtually disappear if you stick with it. Work toward increasing your socialization, and continue engaging in social activities even without the assistance of others. If you are able to commit yourself to a social activity at least once a week, you will be happier and less shy, and, hence, will enjoy a higher quality of life.

6.

Awkward Silences

Awkward silences in conversation are a real bane to shy people. One of my clients disclosed to me that he had been extremely shy growing up and throughout his adulthood. He would often find himself in the middle of a conversation that would invariably end up in one of those long, awkward pauses. Shy people tend to remember those awkward silences and exaggerate their significance and length. Even if a pause in a conversation lasts for only a few seconds, to a shy person it can feel like a lifetime. This isn't just a shy person's problem, either: most people have encountered this conversational problem at least once in their life.

If you find yourself stuck in an awkward silence with someone, extend a friendly gesture such as a smile and a nod; then, when the time is right, simply change the subject. Or, you can always ask a casual question such as, "Oh, where did we leave off?" or just laugh to break the silence. Another direction to take, if you are truly concerned, is to ask, "Did I say something wrong or offensive?"

When an extremely shy person feels unable to hold someone else's interest in a conversation, his or her anxiety will increase in direct proportion to the length of the pause. If this happens to you, try to think positive thoughts. Although you may feel a strong desire to flee the scene, don't. Not all awkward silences are bad; in fact, a pause can be a great opportunity to process information or transition to another topic.

If you're wondering what happened to my client who suffered from those awkward pauses—well, he overcame his shyness after opening his own restaurant. As the owner, he found that he had no choice but to communicate with people constantly. Having to communicate with others to run the business successfully acted as a kind of exposure therapy for him.

Exercise

Think about an interest that you would like to share with others. Then think of some popular topics for small talk that might be interesting to others. Practice with your friends or family members by calling them up and filling them in on the latest news in your life. If you find yourself caught in a moment of silence, try counting to 10 in your head. Most likely, if you wait that long, someone else will speak. The burden is *not* on you to fill the awkward pauses with scintillating small talk. If you're at the office, a great "out" is to say that you need to get back to work or attend to something pressing.

Remember that hitting a lull in the conversation doesn't in and of itself mean that you're hopelessly shy. In this case, overcoming your shyness is just about being prepared and learning how to deal with those pauses comfortably.

7.

Awkward Situations

Shy people tend to avoid awkward situations such as going to new places or meeting new people. I had one client who felt awkward on a daily basis, especially at work, even though he loved his job and had been doing it well for several years. He felt insecure and often felt left out of conversations when the topics didn't apply to him.

If you are feeling awkward in a familiar environment such as work, try thinking of relevant topics you can use as conversation-starters with the people around you. Sharing the intentions and goals of the group—say, by working in the same company and trying to reach the same sales objectives—can increase your social satisfaction.

Sometimes we tend to "mind read" or worry about what to say, and both of these habits can hinder our engagement in a conversation. Mind reading is not necessarily a bad thing, but it becomes a problem when we start interpreting people's motivations negatively all the time. If you assume that people are thinking negative thoughts about you, you will only get more anxious. Moreover, when you imagine that everyone thinks badly of you, you are more likely to behave that way.

Shy people often become observers instead of just enjoying and being in the moment. Try to enjoy the moment without thinking about who is watching you, by engaging in on-the-job activities such as holiday parties and potlucks. Avoid the temptation to leave an event when you feel awkward. You're more likely to regret it later, when you realize that you didn't seize the opportunity to make new friends. Even if you feel too shy or awkward to speak up in a group, take part in the conversation nonverbally by smiling, laughing, and nodding. Eventually you may reach a point where you feel more comfortable speaking.

Exercise

When you are about to speak up in a group, *relax*. Don't forget to take long, deep breaths. A helpful technique is a form of deep-muscle relaxation in response to anxiety. When you feel shy and you start to tense up, try tightening all your muscles and then relaxing them for 10 seconds. Really feel the difference between having tense muscles and relaxed muscles. Artificially creating this disparity between "tense" and "relaxed" can condition you to create and embrace the feeling of relaxation when you are stressed. Another technique is to visualize at least two relaxing scenes clearly for 10 seconds or until you feel relaxed and less shy.

8.

Become a Rabid Sports Fan

Have you ever been at a sports bar during the Super Bowl or a playoff game? Everyone is yelling and screaming, sometimes crying, and always laughing. Do you think they all knew each other beforehand and arrived together on a tour bus? Most were likely complete strangers with just one thing in common: their team. If you're a sports fan, even if you're shy, you will be embraced with abandon, so long as you cheer loudly. What a fun way to help you overcome your shyness! If you're not all that into sports, this one may not work for you; but if you are, this is a surefire way to help you come out of your shell, make new friends, and enjoy an afternoon or evening.

The hard part is getting yourself to go in the first place. All the roadblocks that keep you from engaging with the world will still be present: you don't want to go alone, strangers make you nervous, what could you possibly have to say to people you don't know, *ad nauseum*. The solution is simple, if not easy: talk sports. Read up on the teams first if you need to, so you have something to say. Besides, there is no judgment in these places—all of that energy is going to the game.

If you go at the start of the season, the crowd will be smaller. That may or may not make it easier for you. More people will join in as the season progresses. As the playoffs approach, the crowds get bigger, louder, friendlier, and more into the games. By that time you will have made a few new friends to cheer with. If your home team is in the championships, you have just made a room full of friends that you won't feel shy around, because everybody is enjoying him- or herself too much to feel foolish or awkward.

Yes, there will be awkward moments—after all, that's life—but for the most part you become one of the fans, and that creates an instant and lasting bond. You would be amazed at how open and friendly people can be in these social situations. At least give it a chance. Pick the sport of the season, or wait for your favorite. But go. Not only will you help heal your shyness, but you'll have a good time, too. Even if you only really hang out during the season, the friendship will always be there, waiting for the next season to start. Just because you only see people part of the year does not diminish the friendship or the gift of helping you bring more human contact into your world.

9.

Being Self-Critical

Once upon a time your shyness actually helped you. Perhaps, at one point in your life, you chose to be low-key or retiring, to hang back and observe rather than engage, and it protected you from a bad or dangerous situation. And so you kept the attitude, even when it no longer served you. This is something many folks have had to go through, and it can be very difficult to experience, but it can also be healed.

If you have been shy since, well, forever and want to change that, it's not going to help you one bit if you dwell on how your shyness has negatively impacted your life. If it were something you liked about yourself, you wouldn't be trying to change it. Accept that being shy is something that has held you back, knowing that *now* you are choosing to overcome that fear of social judgment.

We can all be overly self-critical, especially when we realize in retrospect that we could have been a little more engaged in the world and all its diversions. Luckily we can learn from our mistakes and do better next time. Opportunities abound, so don't take yourself to task if you miss a few. Again, sometimes it's good to be cautious. It can help you avoid bad situations and people. As the saying goes, it's better to walk around a tar pit than through it. You are not wrong or bad for making sure you will be safe in any given situation, but once you know you will not in fact be abducted by aliens at the next office party, maybe you'll go and see if you can't have a good time.

Exercise

Some people appreciate self-deprecation and the humility it implies, but others will take you at your word and wonder why you think so poorly of your-self. The next time you hear negative things about yourself come out of your own mouth, silently tell yourself to knock it off. Realize you were talking about your imaginary evil twin, and let it go so that you can re-engage with the people you were talking to. This may take a little practice, but it can be done by anyone with a little self-awareness. By catching yourself before you put yourself down (internally or externally), you will be putting a stop to that negative self-talk cycle, and therefore you'll be able to enjoy the moment as well as your life and the people in it to a greater degree. It is a healing tool for shyness that goes way beyond the fear of social judgment; it makes you a more genuine person and allows you to share the best parts of yourself, because you will no longer feel the need to hide.

It all starts by not allowing the unhealed parts of your mind to control your thinking and what comes out of your mouth. Simply put, if you can't say something nice about yourself, don't say anything at all.

10.
Best Topics for Light Conversation

If you are shy, you probably have a lot of difficulty participating in casual conversations. Perhaps you don't know what to talk about even when there's already a topic at hand. And when you don't know anything about the topic, it can be downright intimidating. I once worked with a client who was extremely shy and who felt insecure when she was out with her boyfriend, who worked in the film industry. He and his friends would discuss technical issues pertaining to their jobs. Because these particular challenges were unrelated to her career, and because she had no knowledge of or experience in their field, she would often find herself feeling inferior and frustrated.

If you are shy and find yourself in a conversation that you can neither relate nor contribute to, one thing you can do is listen carefully and participate nonverbally through nods, smiles, and welcoming eye contact. This lets other people know that you're interested in the discussion, even if you can't add much to it. Another way you can participate is by asking questions. You'd be surprised how excited people get about sharing their knowledge. Look interested in the topic, and engage in the conversation, if you can, by saying something positive. Don't be embarrassed to admit that you don't know anything about the topic at hand. People who are afraid to let others know that they don't understand something are more likely to feel rejected or left out.

The best and safest topics for light conversation are things like the weather or a local restaurant. These topics don't require you to be an expert in anything. It doesn't take much effort to check the news and keep updated on current events and goings-on in your neighborhood. If you stay abreast of local and world events and share your thoughts on them with others, you'll be perceived as a good conversationalist. Everyone likes to learn something new, so try to mention things that will make you shine.

Exercise

Try acclimating yourself to engaging in light and casual conversation. A great place to do this is in a coffee shop. While you're reading a book or working on your computer, make eye contact with someone nearby and give him or her a nonverbal greeting such as a smile or a nod. Once you've practiced this and you want to challenge yourself, ask the person sitting next to you an innocuous question such as "What time is it?" or "How is your day going?" If you find you have more to say, by all means, keep the conversation going. You may still feel shy, but guess what? You've just engaged in a conversation with a stranger!

11.

Being Shy as a Couple

When I work with shy couples, I often find that they are both afraid to express their needs, desires, and feelings to each other. Shy people may fear expressing themselves to their loved ones because they have become emotionally cut off from one another. One couple I worked with had been married for more than 10 years, and their communication had declined to the point that their feelings were no longer being expressed at all. During therapy, I had each of them express their feelings and thoughts to the other. I had them turn to face each other and look into each other's eyes while saying what they wanted and how they felt. I did this because using "I statements"—*I feel, I want, I think*—while looking someone in the eye helps us validate our feelings.

Expressing emotions is difficult for shy people. Expressing negative emotions such as anger and sadness to a significant other can be especially difficult when the relationship is new. However, you can help foster emotional intimacy by using those "I statements." Always end on a positive note. For example, after stating your feelings, acknowledge what it is that your partner is doing right. This way, your partner does not feeling completely invalidated or unappreciated.

Research has shown that if a reward is given too soon, it reduces the duration and intensity of dopamine activity in the brain. (Dopamine if the stuff that signals pleasure to the brain.) The longer it takes to get a reward, the more dopamine the reward produces, and, therefore, the more we appreciate it and try to obtain it. Therefore, relationships that are formed too quickly, in which the partners didn't really get to know each other beforehand, can be difficult to maintain. This is especially true when shyness is a factor. Learning to communicate effectively can increase the partners' positive interactions, though.

Exercise

If you have a routine that you are accustomed to, include your significant other in it. Try initiating a date night, and agree beforehand not to bring up anything that could be considered negative. During tense moments, try using "I statements" to see whether they help defuse strong emotions. Also, try to give each other some space. You might do this by spending a bit of down time with friends and family. This can create a healthy space and help the two of you come back together with newfound understanding and respect.

If you are shy, and you find it really difficult to open up and find positive ways to communicate with your significant other, you might want to suggest couples therapy. It provides a safe and controlled environment in which to say the hard things that need to be said.

12.

Body Language

Approximately 80 percent of our communication is accomplished through body language. When you talk to other people, pay attention to their body language as well as your own. Can you recognize signs of interest (or lack thereof) in the other person's body language? If you yourself are shy, do you use body language that might be interpreted as disinterest? Make mental notes about the kind of body language you are presenting. Are your arms crossed in front of you? Are you hands planted on your hips? Both can come off as disrespectful.

Many shy people have a hard time standing upright, facing the other person, and making eye contact. If you tend to slump your shoulders and avoid eye contact during conversations, redirect those behaviors. When your shoulders start drooping, push them back and up. If you find yourself looking down or away from the other person, make a point to engage in friendly eye contact. (But don't stare, as this can be perceived as hostile.) Ask yourself how you would feel if someone refused to make eye contact with you. If you find it off-putting or rude, others may feel the same way when you do it. You may be giving off a signal that you're not interested in what they're saying, even if you really are.

Another big one is posture. Did you know that you can increase your positive feelings *toward others* by practicing good posture? Simply standing up straight with your shoulders back can increase self-esteem because it lowers cortisol levels and boosts testosterone. And, when you feel good about yourself, you are more likely to feel good about others!

Exercise

If you tend to look down or away from the person you're speaking to, try this exercise. The next time you are speaking to someone, make eye contact with him and hold it while silently counting to 10. After 10 seconds, look away for a moment. Throughout the conversation, remain mindful as to how often and how long you are keeping or avoiding eye contact. Making eye contact for too long can seem rude, but avoiding eye contact altogether can be a sign of disinterest or insecurity.

Here are a few more tips for maintaining positive body language when communicating with others:

- Maintain respectful yet natural eye contact.
- Keep your arms and legs uncrossed.
- Smile and nod to show agreement.
- Practice good posture to portray self-confidence.
- Shake hands firmly while making eye contact.

Exercise

If you are concerned about your body language during a speech or presentation, do some stretching exercises first. Reach your arms toward the ceiling to release tension in your shoulders. Then, touch your toes, do a few squats, or stretch your arms out like an airplane and rotate them from right to left and back again. Relaxing and stretching the muscles will have an impact on how you feel and, hence, how you look.

Once you have greater command over your own body language, you will know how people are perceiving you, and this will help you feel less shy.

13.

Bone Up on Your Social Skills

Social skills are indispensible in virtually every situation. Society itself is built on these skills, and they are critical to the individual's ability to develop and maintain lasting relationships and to participate in the community. A lack of social skills can contribute to psychological distress (when we feel isolated, for example) and a decrease in self-esteem. We can deal with shyness better if we learn the appropriate social skills. One way to do this is to participate in a healthy "extravert" activity, such as going to a bar, a party, or even the mall, at least once a week. Doing this will bring you into contact with other people and force you practice these skills and make them habitual.

If you know you're going somewhere where there will be new faces, have a plan of action in place on the front end. This plan shouldn't include alcohol, by the way. The consumption of alcohol is the fifth most popular strategy used by shy people to deal with social situations. You may feel you need to have a drink in your hand to fit in, but be wary of using alcohol to ease social tensions, and don't engage in unhealthy behaviors such as substance abuse in order to be more extraverted. To avoid becoming dependent on alcohol, try non-alcoholic beverages. This may feel awkward, but remind yourself that nobody will know what's really in your drink. It's quite cool and unique to be able to enjoy a social event without the use of alcohol.

Lastly, practice your social skills. Introduce yourself to others. Do you have a specific achievement that you are proud of and would like to share with others? Consider whether you would like to tell people about your background. Maybe your parents came from another country and you have a unique story to tell. Think of recent events in your life that you might want to share. Did you just get married, or do you plan on getting engaged? All of these are great conversation starters. If you have children, you can also see whether other people have children, too, and exchange stories with them.

Ultimately, having a plan in place for how you will present yourself socially can ease the tension of feeling shy.

14.

Boost Your Communication Skills

Many shy people feel that their shyness is ruining their lives. Many feel as if they were watching their lives pass them by without ever really living. Solving this problem is just a matter of enhancing communication skills and interacting with the right people. Try befriending people with whom you are immediately comfortable or who have similar qualities. This will make the process so much easier.

Practice listening to yourself when you are talking to others, and try to get rid of habitual conversation fillers such as "um," "like," or "ah." The fewer fillers you use in a conversation, the more confident you will appear. When you are talking to someone and find your mind going blank, ask a follow-up question or repeat the other person's last statement and turn it into a question. This will give you time to think while showing the listener that you are paying close attention.

Empathy is another great tool to help shy people with conversation. Sometimes it's difficult to know how to express empathy appropriately. For example, if I told my friend that one of my family members had been involved in an accident, the question, "Whose fault was it?" would be a non-empathetic response. More empathetic responses could include "Oh no! What happened?" or "I'm so sorry to hear about that. Is there anything I can do to help?" These are all more appropriate things to say.

Exercise

One way to improve your communication skills is to learn to manage your schedule better. If you are often late or cancelling on others, this is an area for you to work on. Being mindful of your schedule before committing to anything is an important communication skill that will allow you to earn your friends' trust and confidence. If someone wants to meet with you, and you can't make it at the allotted time, ask if it's possible to reschedule. Rushing through your plans or arriving at an appointment late will only increase your anxiety. After all, your top priority here is to enjoy the meeting with your friend.

Communication skills will feel more natural when you increase your social activities. Don't limit yourself to just one type of social setting: volunteer, take up a course at your local community college, attend a local meet-up, or join a gym class. Search for plenty of social events to attend, including some that are work-related. If you don't like what you do for a living, investigate a new career and attend networking meetings. Take business cards and be prepared to discuss your interests and skills.

15.

Breathe

You'd be surprised at how many people literally hold their breath when they feel shy, nervous, or anxious. What they don't realize is that by not breathing regularly, they're actually cutting off the oxygen supply to their brain and body, so they are unable to think or respond as well as they would normally. Breathing deeply and regularly can reenergize you and give you that little extra bit of clarity you need. I know this sounds simplistic, but it really works.

There are several ways to take in air that will help you calm yourself. Some of them will serve to reduce shyness and, in some cases, even eliminate it. Basic deep breathing is something that has been around for a very long time. Most people don't fill their lungs to capacity when they breathe, so take a moment right now to see how deep or shallow your own breathing is. When I am at my desk, writing, my breathing is usually calm and regular but definitely not deep. When I purposefully inhale more air, I can feel a bit of tension release from my entire body. (By the way, if you find yourself sighing often, it is a sign that your body wants to release tension, not just air.)

Exercise

Yoga breathing is another great technique. The process is pretty quick, which is great if you are in a situation where your shyness is causing you to want to escape *post haste*. First, inhale slowly through your nose, for about eight to 10 seconds; then, hold your breath for five seconds; last, release your breath through your mouth for as long as you inhaled (eight to 10 seconds). It helps if you see it as filling three chambers in your lungs: the stomach/diaphragm; the chest; then, finally, the upper chest (which doesn't hold a lot, so just a little intake at this point is fine). Release all the air at once, but, again, do it slowly.

Not only will this exercise help calm you and reduce your shyness, but it will also keep you healthier and lengthen your life. This is one of those cases where you just have to try it and see how it makes you feel. If you don't feel better, you may not be doing it right. If at first you don't succeed, try, try again.

It will take some time and practice to reap the full benefits of learning to breathe properly, but once you do, you will have taken a big and effective step toward overcoming your shyness. Now breathe, and just keep breathing.

16.

Call a Good Friend

Friendship is highly underrated. It can be the difference between a life of joy and one of loneliness. For someone who is dealing with acute shyness, making friends can seem next to impossible, because the fear that comes from being shy can cripple you and make you feel incapable of reaching out. There are several things you can do to get past this, and most do not require you to do anything that will increase your anxiety.

If you are feeling shy and just can't bring yourself to go anywhere, pick up the phone and call a friend. It will make you feel better about life and yourself. Hearing the voice of someone you care about, and spending a few minutes getting involved in his or her world, can give you a new outlook on your own. Making this positive, emotional connection may be just what you need to get moving again.

Reliability is the cornerstone of any good friendship. Knowing that you can call and count on someone who will be there for you and who "has your back" is empowering and a great comfort. If are not fortunate enough to have anyone in your life like this at the moment, think back on who has been there for you in the past. What happened to that person or those people? Maybe it's time to rekindle a relationship. You can do this from the privacy of your own home simply by sending an e-mail or a text. It doesn't have to be long or dramatic—just a quick hello to begin the reconnection process.

If you want a friend, learn to be a friend. Giving others what you want to get is the best way to show someone how good of a friend you can be. People generally like us because we like them, so let this person know that you'd like to be friends. By establishing that you are friends, it lets the positive emotions sink in, and as they do, it lessens your shyness. That, in turn, will make you a better friend.

Having a friend who won't judge you can make your life better. Feeling judged is part of the pain that many shy people feel. You need to take the risk of trusting and opening up to someone. Remember that letting out your feelings to a trusted ally is also good therapy.

Deep discussions are a true treasure of friendship. When you know that someone really understands you, it is life enhancing and will make you feel stronger. We all have feelings we need to share so that we can be validated. When you get confirmation that what you are dealing with is real and that your emotions about it are appropriate, you feel better about yourself.

Happiness can come from knowing you have good people in your life. If you don't have a family of your own, having your friends as family is a true privilege. This may feel scary to a shy person, but it is the truth. All you need to do is to pick up the phone or send a note to someone you feel you can trust. Your friendships will grow naturally, and your shyness will be alleviated by it.

17.

Change Your Environment

A change of place can do wonders for your shyness, especially if you find a location that brings you peace of mind. When we are in an environment that makes us feel safe and good about ourselves and our lives, it is much easier to reach out and open up to others.

As an example, I used to have a client who was overly shy when it came to regular social activities. However, being on a cruise ship took away her shyness for some reason. She could interact with others easily and enjoy all that the seven seas had to offer. In short, she was like a different person. Unfortunately, when she returned home, she was still somewhat withdrawn, but each time she took a cruise, she became just a little bit bolder, and that carried over to her regular life.

If you have a place where you feel open and safe and confident, perhaps spending more time in that environment or doing that activity will give you the same thing it gave my client. Having an outlet and being able to "put away" your shyness, even just temporarily, will reduce your overall shyness factor each time you engage in it. And, slowly but surely, you will reduce the fear that keeps you from connecting with others.

Changing your environment can help you in other ways, too. For example, if you have a meeting coming up that you are nervous about, get there early and take a walk around the building first (even if it's your own familiar office building). When you can't get your mind clear, sometimes stepping outside can give you a new perspective. Getting some fresh air will enliven your senses and force your brain to start thinking of something more pleasant than the meeting. Changing the environment reduces your anxiety about the meeting, and you will be less shy and better able to participate in the ways you need to.

Another way to change your environment (and develop yourself as a person in the process) is to take some kind of workshop, class, or seminar that requires you to go someplace new. Doing new things actually increases production of the brain chemical oxytocin, which contributes to feelings of safety. The growth you get from your experience will help broaden your horizons, and you will most likely enjoy yourself and maybe even make a new friend or two in the process.

A change of environment can work wonders. It almost always reduces shyness because your mind is busy taking in the new surroundings; you just don't have time to think about withdrawing or wanting to leave the room. It also lowers stress and gives you more to talk about when you meet someone you want to connect with.

18.

Change Your Thoughts, Change Your Shyness

You probably spend a lot of time thinking about how shy you are. This can be counterproductive. When you find yourself dwelling on the very existence of your shyness, try to think about the things you can do to reduce it instead. Antecedents can be helpful in this regard. Antecedents are events that result in either reinforcement or punishment after a particular behavior has occurred. You can use antecedents to increase desired behaviors and prevent the problematic ones from recurring. In short, you can use your experiences to teach yourself to focus on beneficial behaviors and lose the ones that aren't helping you.

If you are shy, you may find it difficult to read other people's feelings. You may also be embarrassed about showing emotions; you may even avoid doing so altogether. However, being able to express emotions appropriately is a necessary part of human interactions, so you'll need to change your thinking about this in order to get your emotions to follow suit. Try attending an event or a class—a dance class, for example—for yourself, based on your own needs and for the purpose of improving your social skills. Don't worry about being the new person in the class. When I took my first tango class, many people were eager to hear about my interest in it, and I had several good conversations and made some new friends.

Finally, before attending your class or event, relax. Use relaxation techniques such as deep breathing before you leave the house, and visualize yourself having a great time. *Tell yourself that you are not shy* and that you are proud of yourself for attending the event you've chosen. Remember: wherever your thoughts go, your emotions will go, as well.

19.

Comparison Is a Confidence Thief

Life is like an onion; you peel it off one layer
at a time, and sometimes you weep.
—Carl Sandburg

This competitive world often encourages—no, demands— that we compare ourselves with others. Unfortunately, this can result in low self-esteem, social withdrawal, extreme shyness, and even self-hatred. Shy people tend to do this more often than most people, which only serves to increase their agony. You can reduce or eliminate this contributor to your shyness by learning to be more comfortable in your own skin. Much of this will involve learning to stop the comparisons. If you think that everyone around you is perfect (which they are *not*), you will never accept your own imperfections.

A client, Sandra, said that she had always been shy and didn't have many friends. In session, she would recall how her brother had been her only friend growing up. She also mentioned that she'd always felt that everyone around her had a better life than she did. Even as an adult, she would focus on the fact that her brother was happily married with a son, while she was still single. The more she compared herself to others, the worse she felt about herself. I helped Sandra see herself, and her accomplishments, individually and not just in comparison to others. Once she could do this, she felt better about herself and started to focus on her blessings.

She was initially enthusiastic about her homework assignment, which involved a making a list of positive attributes and writing a letter of appreciation to herself. However, she was unable to complete the exercise on her own, so she had her parents help her. This exercise helped her to gain insight and helped her to realize how lucky she was. She felt grateful for the life she had and for her parents, who were supportive of her. While reading the letter her parents wrote, Sandra cried and said how grateful she was to know that her parents were proud of her. Sandra had learned the importance of focusing less on others' successes and more on her own. From that moment on, she started to take charge of her life, and her inner self-comparison narrative decreased. As a result, her self-esteem rose, and her shyness slowly started to diminish.

If you tend to compare yourself with others, you've probably noticed an increase in your feelings of insecurity when you indulge in this behavior. If you find yourself doing this, remember that it only creates unnecessary stress and anxiety, and unhealthy feelings such as jealousy, envy, or disappointment. Constant comparison was the main cause of Sandra's depression, anxiety, and shyness, to the point that she was no longer aware of the consequences. After Sandra realized that she had gotten caught in a rut and was only hurting herself, she started to take control of her life, looking at it individually rather than through the distorting lens of comparison.

If you stop comparing yourself to others, you will be free—free to be proud of your own accomplishments, and free from the debilitating effects of the shyness that comes from comparison.

20.

Cultivate Self-Awareness

Knowing who you are is one of the keys to overcoming shyness. Self-awareness is a powerful force when it comes to dealing with the world and its inhabitants. When you know what works for you and what doesn't, and you understand how to make your life count for something (if that's what you want), you have the power to blast shyness from your behavior pattern forever. Are you able to overcome your shyness when necessary, or does it win most of the time? Having that awareness gives you a starting point from which you can make the strides necessary to overcome your shyness. Look at your current ability to put yourself out there and set a goal for where you would like to be in the future.

Part of cultivating self-awareness is to familiarize yourself with your cognitive and behavioral patterns, your habitual responses to people and events. One trick is to have a list of responses ready for common triggers for your shyness. So let's say that when someone asks you a favor, your typical, habitual response—your default response—is to always say yes. If you know this about yourself, you can come up with some alternative replies to the request ahead of time that will help you respond rather than react. So next time, perhaps you'll know to say, "I'll think about it and get back to you," which gives you more freedom and self-assuredness in the moment. Knowing who are by knowing your responses, not reactions, to life's obstacle course helps you get through it more gracefully. And you will feel better for it.

Self-awareness is also about knowing other peoples' boundaries and limitations as well as your own. This is important because you will judge yourself according to the behaviors of others, especially if they can do something you can't and vice versa. Sometimes knowing when you are at your best during the day can help. I write best in the mornings, so I spend most of them in front of the computer doing just that. If I'm on a tight deadline and know that I have to see clients in the morning and thus be forced to write in the evening, it can create anxiety (a trigger for my shyness) that I will feel all day long and which prevents me from being present for the people who need me. Because I know this about myself—there's that self-awareness at work again—I get up a little early and make sure that I create my prose before I have to leave for the office. Sometimes it is that simple, but not all the time.

Self-awareness is a process that can take many years to acquire, so don't think it's something you can attain from reading one chapter in a book. There are many fine works out there that can teach you much more about this complex topic, but the real knowledge is within you.

21.

Depression and Shyness

Depression is often mistaken for shyness. Depressed people are less likely to socialize with others, and this is sometimes perceived simply as shyness. Worldwide, however, depression is a serious and disabling public health problem. Women are twice as likely as men to suffer from depression.

Depressed patients sometimes cease to take part in activities that used to give them pleasure. If you are shy and also suffer from depression, you may feel a persistent low mood accompanied by low self-esteem and a loss of pleasure or interest in things that you once enjoyed. If you feel depressed, take up activities that can alleviate your depression until you feel comfortable enough to socialize. Shyness can also prevent you from telling others what makes you happy, which can make you even more depressed due to the lack of acknowledgment. So it's often a vicious circle. If you feel stuck in a morass of negative thoughts and feelings, you might consider doing cognitive behavioral therapy (CBT), which aims to make you aware of your thought distortions and how those distortions are causing you psychological distress.

Exercise

Try keeping a journal to identify triggers that elicit anxiety or depression or otherwise put you in a low mood. Then, when you start to feel this way, do something relaxing that you enjoy, such as listening to your favorite soundtrack or looking though treasured photos. You could also treat yourself to your favorite food, dessert, or drink. Invite a friend to join you at local museum exhibit or art reception. Record in your journal how effective these measures are in alleviating the bad feelings. If you're having trouble, think of three special moments when you were completely happy. Now think of what you would need to do to be that happy again. Then, do it!

Being shy can really get in the way of being happy. If you find yourself stuck in depression or unable to find relief from feelings of hopelessness and despair, please don't keep those feelings to yourself. Talk with someone—a friend, a confidante, anyone with an empathic ear—or, better yet, with a therapist who is well-versed in these challenges. There is hope!

22.

Display Kindness

Some people believe that being kind is a weakness. Nothing could be further from the truth! Kindness can make the difference between success and failure. It can make your life and relationships deeper and more meaningful. It can also change the lives of others in a very profound and positive way. Kindness is a powerful tool that will help deliver you from shyness and open doors to a life that is filled with warmth.

Some people cover up their shyness with a surly attitude, which only serves to push people away (just what the shy person thinks he or she wants). As you can see, this creates the opposite effect of what the shy person really desires. This is what fear of judgment from others does to us. It causes us to make inappropriate choices and exhibit behaviors that keep others at a distance. By being kind, you open up all kinds of doors and maybe even a few hearts. People will respond in kind by making you feel safe with them. This is easy to understand, but can be a challenge for someone who is used to hiding from the human race, even if you aren't being rude and obnoxious (another tool that helps shy people avoid face-to-face contact).

In order to display kindness, you have to know what it feels like to be on the receiving end of it. So a little homework is in order here. First, think about a few times when people were kind to you; list them, describing what was said or done each time and how it made you feel. (It's helpful to write it all down because while you are composing, other memories and thoughts will come into your head.) Then describe a few separate instances when you were kind to someone else. Take a couple of days with this—it isn't a race. Once you get both lists completed, look at the length of each. Are they equal, or does one vastly outweigh the other? Have you put out more kindness than you have received? Or is it the other way around? If it looks as though you have been the giver primarily, consider the people you have been giving your best self to. Perhaps they are not firmly on your team or are holding a grudge against you. Conversely, if you've been getting much more than you have been giving, it's time to balance the books and start putting out more kindness.

Helping little old ladies (or men) across the street is one way of showing kindness. So is working with people who have developmental problems, tutoring underprivileged kids, and helping the homeless. Don't expect any of the people you are helping to be your friends. This is a one-way street: you give, and they receive. It will positively affect your personality and lessen your shyness. By extending yourself to others you open up a silent path that says, *Hey, I'm a good person, and I am willing to treat you well if you do the same for me.* It's all internal, but these kind of nonverbal messages can speak very loudly to the right people, the people you need in your life.

23.

Dogs Help Heal Shyness

Owning a dog can make a big difference in terms of how you view and deal with your shyness and the world. Research tells us that a dog can make a great deal of difference in how people cope with and overcome their shyness. Additional studies have shown that you appear more likeable if you appear with a dog in a photo than you would if you were holding flowers. My dog appears with me on my business cards, on my Websites, and in the main photo for my blog on Psychologytoday.com. As of this writing, that blog has gotten 10 million views, and I'm sure Mercy's picture has had something to do with that. Following are some of the ways in which having a dog can help you if you're shy.

First, dogs can help you be more social. My dog goes with me everywhere, and she is so cute that someone almost always makes a comment about her. In these cases, I find it easy to engage in light conversation because I'm talking about the dog and not myself. My shyness seems to go away.

Second, dogs pretty much force you to get out of the house. That's one of the best reasons for having one. My little rescue pup loves to go for walks, and even though I have my lazy days when I just don't want to leave the house, knowing that our walk makes her happy is enough motivation to get me up and out, at least for a walk around the block.

Third, by getting out and walking more, you meet more people and socialize more. I'm always talking with other people who are out walking their own dogs. We let the little critters check each other out, and the humans get to exchange a few words as well. As an added bonus, the exercise you are getting will help quell your anxiety, which is at the root of your shyness. When you're ready, go to a dog park where the puppies play and the people sit on benches and talk to each other.

Finally, dogs provide love and relief from loneliness, and are great stress relievers. It is well-documented that simply petting or holding a dog or cat can lower one's blood pressure. A pet's unconditional love helps us relax and makes us feel stronger. I know many shy people who are enjoying life more because of their dog.

I realize that not everyone likes dogs or can have one in their life. Living restrictions, finances, time, and so on are all good reasons to be houndless, but the advantages for those of us who deal with shyness far outweigh any drawbacks. For example, I have a friend who can't keep a pet at her apartment, but she is a total animal lover, so she volunteers at the local animal shelter. She has met a lot of people this way, has helped a lot of animals, and really enjoys her time there. I think it's a creative way of getting your "doggie fix" and mixing with people at the same time.

Exercise

Take a trip to the local pet shop when they have adoptions days—usually on the weekends—or go to an animal shelter, and just bond with the animals. Take note of your feelings and anxiety level both before and after you go. Did you find that holding, petting, or just looking at the animals made you feel better? Did it help alleviate your shyness when interacting with the workers and volunteers? If so, maybe getting a pet would be a great solution for you!

Even if there is a good reason why you can't own a pet, there are always ways around it. If dogs aren't your thing, just about any animal will provide you with the same kind of emotional support. Please visit your local shelter and give yourself the opportunity to see if this works for you. If your heart doesn't melt, you may not have one!

24.

Don't Be Inhibited by Your Past Choices

Sometimes our shyness causes us to make decisions that we later find embarrassing. Perhaps you couldn't bring yourself to go to a friend's wedding or decided to bail on an important gathering because you didn't feel comfortable meeting new people, and now you think the ones who invited you are offended. It's hard when you feel you're being scrutinized and judged for your social choices.

Another way this can manifest in your life is an ex or former partner who is "trash talking" you. This is a hard one to overcome. If you rush in and try to do damage control with the people he or she has been talking to, it can make you look overly defensive, as though you were trying to hide something. And sometimes things are so off-balance that your old friends have taken the side of your ex, so not only do you feel you look bad, but you can't talk to the very people who used to care for you and who need to be enlightened as to the truth. This is a big dilemma, and for a shy person, it can be a trigger that just makes you want to run and hide.

Giving it some time to let the wounds heal on both sides may be your best choice. Even though you miss and need your friends, if someone decides that he or she doesn't want to be there for you anymore, there is very little you can do about it. The fear is that you will be all alone; the reality is that you don't want people in your life who don't completely believe in you. Hold fast to those who do, and use the tools you are learning in this book to help you create more supportive friendships. Someone who leaves your life just because your ex or another person has complained (or lied) about you is not a person who really had your back to begin with. Of course, what this friend *should* do is to give you a call and say, "I heard some things about you that I find upsetting, and I'd like to discuss this with you so we can maintain our friendship." Unfortunately, most people cling to the toxic gossip because it's more dramatic and gives them something on which to focus their own unhealed emotions.

Remember, too, that your old friends may have their own agendas. Maybe they wanted to be with you in some way but were jealous of your past relationship or maybe they envy your current lifestyle and successes. People can get really petty when they don't get what they want. Understanding this and knowing that you're not the problem will give you the strength you need to move on and create the kind of friendships you deserve, with people who will not turn on you.

You did what you did; it's in your past and you can't change it. What you can do now is make things as good as they can be from here on out.

25.

Don't Be Shy— Be Happy!

According to scientists, happiness is a critical factor in mental health. It is a goal not only for individuals, but also for society as a whole. Happiness is strongly associated with agreeability and self-esteem, but if you are shy, you may feel not as happy as others, because low self-esteem is strongly associated with shyness.

When my clients are unhappy and suffering from depression, I ask them to recall their activities that week and list some things they've done that have made them happy. I often find that my unhappy and depressed clients are not socializing regularly. One of my current clients (we'll call him David) has little motivation to be social. In the course of therapy, he has realized that when it comes time to attend an event, he starts thinking of all the burdens it involves, such as driving in traffic, looking for parking, and waiting in lines. If you think of a social event as a task similar to doing the laundry or going to the dentist, of course you will make excuses to not go out. David needs to realize that viewing a social event as a task will only make him more likely to stay home and remain isolated and unhappy. Oftentimes, the hardest part of attending a social event is just getting there.

Happiness is both a practice and a habit. If you want to be happy, you need to try to avoid any thoughts that might interfere with that, even thoughts of your own shyness. When David would imagine all the steps he had to go through to attend a social event, he was actually creating negative associations that would further reinforce his choice to avoid social events in the future. These associations provide ready-made excuses for shy people. But we have more control over our happiness than we think; it all starts with positive thinking and a little effort.

Ultimately, we will only make ourselves unhappy by avoiding social events. If time is really your issue, think up a new routine that will let you attend the event. There is probably a cafe or a store in the area that you've always wanted to check out. You can stop in there if you arrive early and have some extra time. The more we isolate ourselves, the more we become conditioned to being alone. In order to break that cycle, we almost have to force ourselves to attend events. If that's what it takes, attend as many events as you can until you start to feel satisfied with your life. The more often we socialize, the sooner we become conditioned to socializing, resulting in an increase in our happiness and self-esteem.

Exercise

Brainstorm some ways you could increase your happiness that would also reduce your shyness. For example, think about reducing your negative self-talk regarding social events. If you say to yourself, *It will take forever to get there; plus, I'm sure the traffic will be horrendous*, this negative thought will keep you from enjoying the event—and your life—to its fullest. Make positive statements instead, such as, *I can't wait to see [the event, person, or venue]* or *This will be exciting, and I'll be able to make new friends!* Once you're there and enjoying yourself, you might forget that you ever felt shy about it, which in turn will create a positive association with going out.

26.

Don't Catastrophize

Low confidence and shyness can result from past disappointments. If you've allowed past failures or upsets to dictate your behavior, you may be engaging in *cognitive distortion*. Cognitive distortion is an unhealthy way of thinking that involves exaggerated and irrational thoughts. According to theorists, these thoughts can perpetuate certain psychological disorders. If you end up disappointed or upset by something or someone, try not to catastrophize the event. Try to reduce your negative thinking by looking at the glass as half-full instead of half-empty. Fact is, we all have to go through trials and tribulations at some point in our lives. What is important is how we react to those times.

If you keep thinking that things are either all good or all bad—"This *always* happens to me," or "I *never* have any luck"—try to refute this unhealthy type of black-and-white thinking by being more understanding and flexible in your thoughts. For example: "It didn't work out last time, but there's no reason it can't be different in the future." Another way to redirect your thinking is to ask yourself what positive things you gained from the negative experience. It is said that what doesn't kill you makes you stronger, so praise yourself for the strength and wisdom you gained from your bad experience. Using what you've learned to help others is another way to turn that negative thinking, that catastrophizing, on its head.

27.

Don't Give Up on Yourself

Many shy people give up trying to overcome their shyness and fall into a life of loneliness and quiet desperation. The need for companionship is very human, very normal, and very necessary. It gives us emotional balance and lets us enjoy life. It is also in our DNA, so to deny that fact isn't facing reality.

Staying in denial about what you need to be happy or merely content won't help. Getting past your shyness is something that you should do for yourself, but not completely on your own. There are countless people out there—professionals, friends, family, even pets—who can help. But you are the one who needs to ask for help, who gets the process started *and* keeps it going.

At times you will feel like giving up. You will say to yourself that life alone is not what you want, but that you will accept it and find a way to deal with it, or you'll simply learn to mask the pain. Unfortunately, too often that leads to unhealthy choices such as self-medication with drugs and/or alcohol. Know that self-medicating will only make you feel worse in the end; it may damage your health and even end your life prematurely.

Let's agree on one basic premise: it is better to be here, even if you are lonely, than not. As well, a lonely life is better than no life at all or one spent in a gulag. When you realize that things could be much worse, it helps give you some perspective and helps you appreciate what you have, which in turn gives you the desire to make it even better. We all have moments of wanting to give up, not just on ourselves, but on having a full life. You need to become unwilling to accept that you are destined for sadness and that there is nothing you can do to eliminate your shyness. That is untrue, plain and simple.

Yes, it is okay to have moments or even some days when you just want to hide under the covers. That, too, is very normal. But you need to use every ounce of energy you have to pull yourself out of it and start making your life better again. It can only happen if you continue to look for new and different ways to alleviate your shyness to the point that socializing with others becomes just a normal part of your life and doesn't fill you with anxiety.

If you've been resigning yourself to a life that is only half lived, it is time to reach out. If you have family, call them or go over and see them; if you don't have family, try a friend; if none is available, see a therapist. You need to start talking about how you feel and ask others how *they* think you are doing with your life and struggle. By getting this kind of emotional support and feedback, you are breaking the negative cycle and allowing yourself to move forward again.

28.

Don't Hide

If you want to overcome your shyness, you need to get out there so that people can see that you exist. Some people will want to help, while others may even be detractors, but if you don't make it known that you are here and want to be more involved with people and with life, nothing will change. I know how hard it is to put yourself in front of others. It's almost impossible for some, but you don't have to make a speech or be on stage for people to notice you. Many successful and happy people have found ways of letting others know they are available to participate in various aspects of life.

Ask yourself if your shyness is causing you to hide from the human race. If you just go to work, run errands, and race home, how will you ever meet anyone? Even if you are hiding successfully, is that what you really want? People hide when they don't feel safe. Yes, there are people in this world who hurt other people, and that makes life very uncomfortable and scary, especially for a shy person. It also gives almost anyone a good excuse to run away.

Albert Einstein, a very famous—and very shy—person, once said that "we all need to see the universe as friendly." He makes a great point. If you think you are going to get hurt, you will keep looking for that to happen. Even if it doesn't, your time will be ruined because you will always be looking over your shoulder for the other shoe to drop. What has to drop is your fear of humanity, and you can only do that by testing the waters. The good news is that you don't have to do it alone!

Exercise

Start small, maybe by having just a few friends over to your home, or, better still, meet somewhere neutral, because there will be additional members of the human race there, as well. The object of this exercise is to help you enjoy being around other people, so make the process as comfortable for yourself as possible. If that means just having your cousin or a couple of close friends over, that's fine. Pace yourself, and don't push your comfort level too far, too quickly, because that can cause you to regress and want to hide again. You get to call the shots here, and that should make you feel stronger and safer.

Countless people out there experience a similar level of fear when it comes to overcoming their shyness and meeting new people. Knowing you are not alone and having a close friend by your side can make opening up to the world that much easier. You get to take the first step in making yourself more available to others. You get to be in control of when, where, and how that happens. Your shyness may have kept you from enjoying and experiencing life's gifts, but you don't have to stay hidden any longer.

29.

Eating in Public as a Shy Person

A friend of mine revealed that his reluctance to eat in public was a prelude to his developing anorexia, an eating disorder. He added that he had always been shy, and constantly worried about being judged by others on how he eats.

He had no concrete reason to feel this way, but he ended up being unable to eat at social events or in public. He said that whenever he ate out, he felt as though he were under a microscope. If he saw anyone looking his way, he would assume that they were judging his eating habits negatively. Eventually, he started feeling that if he ate less, the judgments would be good.

If you are extremely shy when it comes to eating in public, you should learn more about eating disorders. Online resources such as the National Eating Disorders Association provide information and treatment options for a variety of eating disorders and related issues. Empirical studies have shown that shyness is actually a predictor of substance abuse, mood disorders, and, yes, eating disorders. Likewise, women with eating disorders tend to have more difficulties in social situations.

People who are overweight or have other medical issues can have difficulty eating around others, as well. One client of mine remembers her mother giving her a nice lunch to take to school and then feeling devastated when she discovered that her mother had made her a salad while all the other kids had sandwiches. This increased her shyness and her anxiety about eating in front of others, because she assumed that they were laughing at her because she was too fat to eat a sandwich.

Exercise

If eating around others is causing you anxiety, try some positive self-talk. When you are eating in public, tell yourself *I'm having a great time,* or *The group of people next to me are not paying attention to how I eat,* or *I'm glad I did this.* Try eating dishes that are not too messy or complicated, so you have less reason to worry. If you're going to eat out with friends, look up the menu online beforehand. This way you can go in with some idea of what you'd like to order. If you want to eat healthily, befriend someone who has healthy eating habits and ask him or her to join you for lunch.

Finding ways to make the experience of eating in front of others more comfortable and even enjoyable will go a long way toward helping you become less shy.

30.

Face Your Issues

You've probably already discovered that cutting yourself off emotionally from others reduces your anxiety immediately. But this is a temporary solution, and it ultimately leads to unresolved problems in your life and relationships. Avoidance is a defense mechanism, a tool that we use to protect our ego, reduce anxiety, and prevent discomfort. Shy people tend to avoid facing difficult emotional issues. If you find yourself being avoidant, ask yourself how can you resolve your issues rather than avoid them, because they must be dealt with.

Shy people often tell me that they find it hard to talk about their concerns. In the business world, most communication problems stem from misunderstandings, which can result in accusations and distrust. You may find yourself with an issue like this at your job, but have difficulty bringing it up with others. Your anxiety may stem from uncertainty about how to talk about your problem. Try writing down the issue or issues; then describe how you feel about them and why. Practice different ways of bringing up your concerns to others. Practice on the phone with a close friend, by telling him how and why this issue concerns you. Or practice in front of the mirror, making eye contact with yourself. When you are ready to face the issue with the person or people concerned, remember to consider the context, and what time and place might be the most appropriate.

Assumptions can lead to missed opportunities. We decide not to bother people with our problems because they seem too busy, or because the timing might bad. As a result, we put the issue off until tomorrow. The problem is that tomorrow can quickly turn into next week and next month—or never. It may be easier to broach the topic if you practice a few open-ended sentences or questions that can be used to jumpstart a conversation. Try using phrases such as "In order to improve our business, what would you think about...?" or "How would you feel about considering...?" to engage the other person. Another great option is to simply ask what you can do to help. This lets others know that you are available, and it can open doors to more opportunities. When we are direct, others are more likely to appreciate us and view us as honest and trustworthy.

Exercise

Think of some appropriate ways to open up about an issue or problem you're facing. Ask yourself how important it is to resolve the issue right now, and whether you are taking the right approach with the right person. Remind yourself that only good things can come from exploring an unresolved issue more fully and discussing how you feel about it.

Emotional cutoff is also a tool we use to avoid unwanted feelings, such as anxiety, the pain of rejection, or the fear of social alienation. We often engage in emotional cutoff without consciously realizing it; however, we can know we are doing it simply by looking at how much we are engaging in relationships with our friends and coworkers. For example, if you are being invited to parties, get-togethers, and events, and you decline as a matter of course without even thinking about it, you have probably conditioned yourself to avoid social events. When we open up to others, we form bonds and connections with them. The more we connect with others, the more we'll be invited and included. This can increase our self-esteem and reduce our shyness.

A social function may not be the best place or time to bring up a problem or ask for input, but once you've connected with someone, you can always ask him or her to join you one day for coffee. Starting a light discussion on an issue you are dealing with can open the doors to advice and solutions. Doing it this way enables you to begin what has the potential to be an uncomfortable discussion in a more comfortable and safe context.

31.

Famous Introverts

Courtesy of *Forbes* and the Huffington Post, here is a list of famous people who are/were also shy—just like the 100,000,000 other Americans who deal with this, and millions more around the world. It's an impressive group. Your mission, should you decide to accept it, is to become one of them. You don't have to be an extravert to change the world!

- Albert Einstein: physicist, author of the theory of relativity, awarded the Nobel Prize for physics in 1921.
- Warren Buffett: chairman and chief executive officer of Berkshire Hathaway, Inc.
- Frederic Chopin: 19th-century French-Polish romantic composer.
- Charles Darwin: scientist and author of *The Origin of Species.*
- Mahatma Gandhi: Indian spiritual master and politician.
- Al Gore: former U.S. vice president (and inventor of the Internet!).
- Sir Isaac Newton: physicist and author of the theory of gravity.
- Larry Page: cofounder of Google.
- Rosa Parks: civil rights activist.

- Eleanor Roosevelt: former U.S. first lady and humanitarian.
- J.K. Rowling: British author of the famed *Harry Potter* series.
- Steven Spielberg: director and producer.
- Steve Wozniak: cofounder of Apple.
- Abraham Lincoln: president of the United States and the man who ended slavery in the United States.
- Emma Watson: actor.
- Christina Aguilera: singer, actress, producer.
- Michael Jordan: basketball phenom.
- Gwyneth Paltrow: actor, singer, and entrepreneur.
- Harrison Ford: actor.
- David Letterman: comedian and TV host.
- Bill Gates: cofounder of Microsoft.
- Johnny Depp: actor.
- Courtney Cox: actor.
- Audrey Hepburn: actress (in her day, women never called themselves actors).
- Roy Rogers: actor, singer, cowboy star.
- Candice Bergen: model and actor.
- George Stephanopoulos: news anchor and White House communications director under President Bill Clinton.
- Richard Branson: billionaire CEO of Virgin Airlines.
- Johnny Carson: comedian and iconic TV host.
- Will Ferrell: comedian and actor.
- Lady Gaga: singer and performer.
- Sir Elton John: singer and songwriter.

Even though you may never win a Nobel Prize or the hearts of millions, you can achieve your dreams and do some amazing things simply by knowing that other shy people have made the world a better place to be.

32.

Fear of Saying No

Why is it that two-year-olds have a much easier time saying no than many of us who are much, much older? Shy people can have a great deal of difficulty finding ways to tell the people in their lives that they can't or won't do something.

If your shyness is screaming at you that you are in an uncomfortable situation or conversation, you must learn to protect yourself by learning how to make a graceful exit. For some, refusing a request creates a fear of being ostracized or even hated. This is the kind of insecurity that teenagers and many adults confront when faced with a group of peers who are engaged in behaviors that are less than desirable, such as drinking to excess. This also can be a problem in the workplace when a subordinate feels that his or her job would be in jeopardy if a demand from a superior were not acted upon—even if that order was counterproductive or inappropriate.

People who always say yes—sycophants—usually end up feeling resentful. Such people often suffer from exhaustion because they have allowed themselves to be tyrannized by the needs and desires of others. Because they are so afraid of being asked to do things that are beyond their comfort zone, they often end up isolating themselves from others. The combination of feeling resentful, tired, and alone can lead to depression, so it's important that we all learn our limits and set good boundaries. Following are 10 creative ways to say no that will help you set healthy boundaries and make your life a whole lot easier:

1. Your basic "No, thank you" is usually your best bet when someone is offering something you don't want.

2. Saying "Nice of you to ask, but I really can't" is a polite way of avoiding an uncomfortable request.

3. Offering a rain check (if you want to) is totally fine. Just say, "Not today, but perhaps later in the week."

4. Giving someone direction by saying "Why don't you try asking Mr. Smith? He may be able to help," allows you to contribute something to the person making the request.

5. Practice saying no the next time you get a call from a telemarketer.

6. "That's not part of my job description" (said with humor and a wink) is a great one to use at work when someone makes an inappropriate request.

7. If you're asked out by someone who's not your type, you can say simply "I'm not interested, sorry."

8. "Let me think about it" will put off those wanting something urgently.

9. If you're facing someone who won't take no for an answer, you may need to be assertive or even aggressive to protect yourself. "I already said *no*," uttered forcefully, may work well in this situation.

10. An empathic "I'm so sorry, but I can't right now" is appropriate when you really can't be there for someone whom you care for.

To shore up your boundaries, memorize and use these talking points, and don't feel that you have to be nice to everyone all the time. In the end, you will have closer and more successful relationships, because other people respect those who respect themselves.

33.

Fears, Phobias, and Shyness

Fear can manifest itself at several different levels. For some, fear isn't a big issue; they have the occasional worry but seem to be able to shut it off. For others, feelings of impending doom and anxiety become overwhelming, and the very idea of dealing with other people becomes intimidating. If you are shy, it can be a real challenge to face your fears.

Fear is a natural and normal emotion that keeps us safe in dangerous situations. It releases adrenaline and other chemicals into the brain and body that prepare us to fight or flee the danger. This response came in rather handy in prehistoric days, when we had to outrun saber-toothed tigers and other predators. Unfortunately, in modern times, the same response can stop us from experiencing and enjoying life.

Some fears manifest as phobias. These are powerful compulsions that make people unbearably anxious when they are presented with certain triggers. A fear of heights might make you hold tightly to the handrails of an elevator as it rises to the top of the Eiffel Tower. If you have a genuine phobic response to heights, however, you may experience powerful physiological response and even panic when faced with the proposition of taking the elevator; this response can include such symptoms as rapid heartbeat, sweating, faintness/light-headedness, and nausea. Some people may even cry or become angry at the mere suggestion of going any place high up. Again, this response is typically amplified if you are a shy person.

Luckily, people who confront their phobias can overcome them and their shyness, as well. As with most emotional issues, it's best to begin by talking about the problem. Talking will help you gain some perspective. For example, being afraid of interacting with others is not rational, but it can feel overwhelming, even though you know intuitively that you are safe. You must work through the fear and the shyness by telling yourself that everything is okay and will continue to be.

Being shy and having a phobia can drastically constrain your life. I once worked with three shy people on *The Ricki*

Lake Show. One had a phobia of heights, another, a phobia of flying, and the third, a phobia of dogs. These phobias kept them from attending many events, made friendships difficult, and limited their lives to the point where they know they needed and wanted to do something about them.

Desensitization combined with relaxation works well in overcoming both phobias and shyness. Desensitization involves the patient taking a series of baby steps that gradually move him or her toward overcoming the phobia. On the show, I started with the woman with the fear of heights. First, I had her climb a small step stool, which wasn't a problem for her; then, we moved to a higher platform, where she worked through some genuine tears. Next, after some deep sharing and relaxation exercises, she climbed a ladder. Finally, she culminated her day with a ride in a cherry picker. It was still very scary for her, but this brave woman understood that she had let her fear of heights run her life, and she had decided that it was time to stop.

Examining how our fears hold us back is an important step in overcoming them. I promise you that working through a phobia will empower you in all areas of your life, especially your shyness. Begin slowly and get as much support as you need. Once you face your fears, you will have changed your life forever.

Exercise

Start by calling an old friend or two and chat with them about their lives and yours. The more you talk, the less shy you will feel, so it's important that you don't let your fears keep you from this important exercise. Finish the conversation by making plans to see the person sometime soon.

34.

Feeling All Alone

Mother Teresa once said that "the greatest disease in the West today is not TB or leprosy; it is being unwanted, unloved, and uncared for." Have you ever felt so lonely that you thought your heart would break in two, and that you wouldn't make it through the night? Have you looked at your life and wondered where you went wrong and asked why you deserve to be so alone? Unfortunate circumstances or our own decisions can sometimes put us in a position where we have no one to turn to. Even if your lifestyle is a comfortable one, the pain of feeling unloved can be so overwhelming that you can start to think about not wanting to be here at all.

More suicides take place during the summer, especially in late July and August, than at any other time of year. No one knows why this is the case, but emotional pain seems to be more intense for people at this time of year.

> If you have been thinking about taking your own life, seek help immediately. Please reach out to a friend or family member or call the National Suicide Prevention Hotline at 800-273-8255. There are people there 24 hours a day, seven days a week, who want to help you.

To help you heal from your shyness, it's very important to make connections with other people. Isolating yourself is only going to make you feel worse. I know people who have gotten roommates, just to have another human being in the house, and it has helped. Others who are in need of companionship get involved in community events or go back to school. The idea is to spend time with other people so that you can feel their warmth and let it help you out of your pain. A warm smile from a good friend can make the difference between hiding under the covers and getting out into the world to see what it has to offer. Many folks find that going out is much easier when they have someone there with them.

Texting and e-mailing are helpful, but they can never take the place of a real conversation with a real person right in front of you. I know people who text each other all day long, and they say it makes them feel more connected. Don't get me wrong—I love getting messages from my sweetheart, but it will never take the place of hearing her reassuring voice and feeling her caring touch. If you spend more time in front of a smart phone, computer, or television than you do with your fellow human beings, you are setting yourself up for your loneliness to get worse. It is important for you to get out of your own head for at least a few hours each day.

Life is about balance, and it is important that we learn to take care of ourselves and each other. When you are done reading this section, pick up the phone and call a friend or a relative and make some plans to get together. You and the person you reach will both be better for it.

35.

Find a Wing
Man/Woman

One of the old-fashioned ways of meeting and socializing with other people has become new again, and it
happens to be a great tactic for shy people. (By the way, I
have used this technique myself and it works great—I didn't
feel awkward or out of place at all.) The idea came from
fighter pilots who always fly in formation: one leads, and
the other protects. The protector is called the "wing man."
The way you can use this concept to help expand your social
reach is by asking a good and trusted friend (man or woman)
to go with you to events or parties that you feel too shy to
attend by yourself. The great part about having a wing man
or woman is that you never have to be or feel alone.

For example, if you meet someone new and strike up a
conversation, you will likely experience a moment or two
of uncomfortable silence. Your wing man (or woman) can
then jump in and fill the awkward conversational space. This
helps everyone stay engaged with the interchange; plus, you
don't have to be anxious about what to say next, because your
wing man/woman has your back.

This technique provides the immediate benefit of rescu-
ing you from your current shyness, as well as the long-term

benefit of lessening your overall shyness factor, because you are practicing and getting more comfortable with talking to new people. This is not just an exercise; it is a way of changing your life for the better and putting yourself out there in a way that is comfortable and reassuring. You will also get to know yourself better, which, as you will see, also reduces shyness (see Chapter 20 for more on self-awareness).

Let's say you were invited to a party that you are reticent to attend because of your shyness. Maybe you don't know the host that well, or perhaps the other people who are coming are complete strangers to you. Either of these scenarios can make you want to say "no thanks." Try this instead: ask the person who invited you who else is coming. If you know any of them, call them and ask about going together or carpooling. (You don't have to get into the "will you be my wing man" conversation just yet!) If it turns out that you won't know anyone attending, ask the host or hostess if he or she minds if you bring a friend. It's common practice to bring a companion or even a date to a party, so don't hesitate to ask. Then start calling a few friends and see if anyone would like to go with you. If you find a compassionate friend, you can then explain the wing man concept and ask if he/she would be kind enough to play that role. Most people will be flattered and think it will be fun. And, if your friend truly cares about you, he or she will gladly accept. (By the way, there is a saying among fighter pilots, "Never leave your wing man." So don't abandon him or her at the party!)

36.

Find Your Voice

Shy people are often afraid of appearing aggressive or disrespectful if they speak in a loud or strong tone. When you are speaking, speak confidently. If your tone of voice becomes weak or low, clear your throat and continue. Speak clearly, and ensure that you are understood by enunciating your words. If you are shy, the last thing you want to hear is someone asking you to repeat yourself. If this happens to you a lot, don't worry about speaking too loudly. Speaking up will only help you increase your self-esteem and confidence over time.

If you are shy, you may find direct questions and discussions too intense. Remind yourself that they aren't interrogations. If you find yourself in such a discussion, think of something positive you can do later that day to reward yourself, whether it's dinner or a simple walk or a coffee break. Knowing that you have a reward coming will help you cope with any uncomfortable feelings you encounter.

If you have a meeting or a presentation coming up, it's important to prepare. Even if you're not the one giving the presentation, you can still prepare by reading up on the subject beforehand. If you are presenting and want to reduce your shyness, you can prepare by recording yourself speaking and then listening to it in order to find and strengthen any weak points. Have an extra copy of your presentation on a USB drive or e-mail it to yourself in case you can't bring it up on your computer when you need it. Print out your presentation slides ahead of time so that you can refer to them without looking over your shoulder. Don't forget to bring healthy snacks to boost your energy during breaks. Taking these kinds of preparative actions can go a long way toward buttressing your confidence.

If you're a particularly nervous speaker, pay attention to your breathing. Do you tend to take short, quick breaths? This can result in hyperventilating. Becoming more mindful of your breathing will help give your body and brain the oxygen they need to perform at their peak. If you're mid-meeting and you feel the need to regroup, don't be afraid to stop and calmly say, "Let's take a 10-minute break." This can give you the time you need to catch your breath, literally and figuratively. Take a bathroom break, practice your deep breathing, and splash a bit of cold water on your face. When it's all over, you will feel proud of yourself for having worked through your shyness.

37.

Focus on Your Goals

If you want to overcome your shyness, you may want to set aside few minutes each day to focus on and visualize that goal. Directing your thoughts toward breaking down your shyness barriers will make the goal that much easier to attain. If you consider yourself to be a painfully shy person, this exercise can be especially helpful, because you don't have to put yourself out there right away. You just visualize what it is you want out of life—to be more outgoing, for example—and paint a picture in your brain of what that would look like. Who would you be as a more confident person? Would you change your line of work, start a new business, or climb the corporate ladder? How would you behave differently in social situations? Asking yourself these questions will help you develop a better picture of how you want your life to be.

Exercise

Studies have shown that writing down your goals and reviewing them regularly makes them much easier to reach. Write down your goal, whatever it is, on a piece of paper. Then put it on your desk or tape it to the bathroom mirror—anywhere you'll see it every day. This reminder will act as an affirmation and help keep you focused, even when your life is at its busiest. Remember that the more you think about your direction, the easier it will be to get there.

It's always a good idea to keep your goals achievable. For example, it would be unadvisable to spend your time focusing on becoming a rock star if you can't play the guitar or sing. Make sure that what you want and need are things that you can actually make happen. When you take an honest inventory of your talents and abilities, you will see pretty quickly how far you can go. If you are having a hard time believing in yourself or finding things that you might be good at, you might want to ask a few close friends to weigh in on what they think your most notable abilities are. People who care about us sometimes see things in us that we are unable to see for ourselves.

If you tend to be introverted, your goals may include things like plenty of quiet time or being in peaceful surroundings. Both of these goals are fine, but make sure you aren't coming from a place of fear. Our insecurities can hold us back and make us think we can't do things that we may be more than able to accomplish. If you allow fear to rule you, your entire life will be focused on playing it safe, and you may miss many of the good things that are waiting for you. Don't sell yourself short, and remember that no one can tell you that you can't do something except *you*.

38.

Focus on Something Different

Shyness stops us from doing things we would like to do. It keeps us sitting alone in our room, far from the music, the fun, the interesting stuff of life. It can be a sad life, but it doesn't have to be. Here is a tip that might help you: if you can't go out or do something you'd like to do, look at what's immediately in front of you. Find something else to occupy your thoughts and energy for a little while. It doesn't really matter what it is; the point is to clear your mind by temporarily putting aside whatever is keeping you stuck. Then, check in with yourself and see whether your desire to do whatever it was is still there. You may just feel better about it.

This temporary distraction technique is a way of letting your mind relax long enough for you to shift your thinking. If you've been ruminating on your fear of going somewhere or meeting someone, start by thinking of something else or doing a menial, rote task, such as the dishes. It can help you refocus your thoughts and let the positive ones overpower the negative ones.

Changing how you think and what you think about is one of the most effective tools you have to assist you in overcoming your shyness. In simple terms, if you aren't dwelling on—feeding—your fear, it will go away on its own. By constantly thinking about it, you are actually giving it more power and allowing it to run your life. The truth is that you are stronger than your fear, but you need to learn a few ninja moves to kick it to the curb. Changing your thinking by doing something completely different is a tool that works, but only if you use it.

Exercise

When you are caught in the cycle of fear that is part of your shyness, it can feel next to impossible to *stop* thinking about it. That's why I am stressing that you actually do something about it by picking up a book, cleaning the house, or petting your dog. Focusing on something you love will help a lot. If after that you are still having trouble releasing your insecurity, tell yourself that you don't want to feel this way anymore, and remember a time (maybe yesterday) when you felt stronger. This will help you shift your energy and thinking so that you are more available, mentally and emotionally, to take care of yourself by doing whatever it is that is being hampered by your shyness.

This exercise can become second nature with practice. When I find myself thinking about unpleasant things, I do whatever I can to change my thinking. I simply don't want the feelings that come with the negative thinking, so I have learned to redirect my thoughts. I know you can do it, too!

39.

Get Some Emotional Support

The energy you get from people who care about you is a gift. It's important to remember that people who have close relationships and friendships generally live longer and fuller lives. Most people, when they feel the need, can reach out to someone who cares about them. But for a shy person, this can be a real challenge.

Many people feel as though they simply can't get their lives moving in the right direction. If you embrace the emotional support of those close to you, you will find it much easier to get to where you want to go. Even the most painfully shy person can find someone to talk to, even if it produces a little anxiety at first. But even that can change if the person you are talking to is willing to be supportive. The only way to find out is to make a call or send a text or e-mail. I urge you to pick up the phone in this case, though, as hearing a voice is much more powerful and will give you more support than a written response (which can sometimes be lacking in tone). If the first person you call doesn't answer, call someone else. If you have no one, please make an appointment with a therapist. If you don't know one, call your MD and get a referral. Sometimes just making that first appointment will make you feel better because you are finally moving in a positive direction.

Getting emotional support can be something you can do in a group setting, as well—hence all those support groups out there. If you go to Google and look up support groups in your area, you'll probably be surprised at how many you find. This task may also seem daunting to the very shy, but the truth is that you can hide better in a group than you can when you are one-on-one with someone. Depending on the kind of group, people usually just say hello and take their seats; they may or may not introduce themselves. Often there is a facilitator or a speaker, and the group may engage in an exercise. But I have never experienced a group that forced people to speak if they didn't want to. All you have to say is "I pass," and they will move on to the next person. There is sensitivity in these rooms.

You may eventually feel comfortable enough to share what is going on in your life to the whole group, but this may take attending a few meetings first. What you are looking for is the positive feedback and emotional support that these groups are all about. If someone takes you to task or is unkind, you are at the wrong meeting.

Building an emotional support network is paramount to overcoming shyness. If you don't have one, and you find a support group to attend, please do—it's a great place to start. If you are lucky enough to have a few people in your life who are emotionally supportive, begin to rally the troops and talk with the people who care about you. Just doing this will not only ease the burden you carry, but it will also reduce your shyness.

These tips have helped thousands of people lead fuller lives and discover parts of themselves they have never known. Overcoming your shyness will come from moving yourself forward. Give it a try.

40.

Giving to Others Helps Alleviate Shyness

What you many not know about me is that when I was a young man—a kid, really—I wanted to be a philanthropist. Problem was, I never had enough money to start a foundation so I worked in fundraising for Greenpeace and other nonprofits (in between gigs with my band) until I began my psychology studies. Fortunately my writing gave me a taste of success and allowed me to give a little bit of money to those in need. Writing this and other books has made such a difference because I don't feel that I am completely wasting my life. My hope is that readers will learn from my struggles. It's life, and bad stuff happens to good people all the time. Writing is my way of acknowledging this and giving back—my own unique brand of philanthropy. By giving to my readers in this way, I feel I am doing some good as I stay productive, which also feeds my self-esteem. It can do this for you, too.

If you escape from your worries by writing, as I do, use it both as a healing process and as a way to help others. Sharing your feelings will help you and others, as they are able to relate to and learn from your struggles. All you need to do is find a way to give from your heart that makes you feel better, even braver. Ultimately, it's hard to feel shy when someone or something you care about is in need. Being shy is often a way of avoiding a fear of failure. What you need to remember is that when you are caring for and giving to others, you can never fail.

41.

Help Someone

When it's time to help someone you care about, you'll find that your shyness usually goes away long enough to get the job done. The power of love is strong enough to help us accomplish amazing tasks in spite of ourselves. We have all heard the stories of mothers lifting cars off of their children. They can do this because in the moment of panic, their brain sends a big shot of adrenalin to their body, and they are endowed with almost superhuman strength long enough accomplish this amazing feat.

Maybe getting over your shyness is a matter of getting more involved with a person or cause that needs you. It is very likely that, in the heat of the moment, your brain will send your body the chemicals it needs to overcome (or at least overlook) your shyness long enough to make a difference in someone's life. Making a difference doesn't take a lot of effort; more often than not, it's just about being there for someone.

Little things, like bringing a sick friend some chicken soup or giving someone a lift to the airport, are also helpful, because they get you out and about when you might otherwise choose to isolate. They also make your relationships better because you are doing something that is actually a big part of being a friend. Just by extending yourself to someone in need, you break down the walls of shyness.

It's also great to get involved in your community. I have friends who volunteer at their local animal shelter and they love it. I know others who support Habitat for Humanity and have a blast building houses with complete strangers. These friends are not normally outgoing, but when it comes to lending a hand (or a paw), they come out of their shells. What is it that brings you out of your world? What inspires you to make a difference? When you find something that moves you, get involved, and I can almost guarantee that your shyness will not hamper your ability or your desire to change your life and the lives of others.

Exercise

Go online and look for a volunteer opportunity in your community that appeals to you. Or, call the local senior center and see how you can be of service (sometimes it's easier to be around seniors and kids than your peers). The beautiful part of this healing activity is that you get to pick what works best for you.

Essentially, by helping others, you are also helping yourself. Anyone who has done this kind of thing knows that the payoff is feeling better about yourself. The increase in self-esteem is also an additional shyness smasher, so no matter how you look at it, extending yourself to those in need is a win-win.

42.

How to Know Whether Your Shyness Is Healing

If you've been shy most of your life, it can be hard to recognize when you are actually getting over it. Here are few signs that you are probably on the mend:

- You find yourself singing along with the car radio. Most of the time depressed people don't sing out loud in their cars. When you catch yourself on the freeway pretending you are Pink or Adam Lambert, it could be a sign that you are feeling some happiness. Just notice it and take it in.

- Things that used to scare you don't anymore, or at least not as much. You may find yourself driving to places that you were too overwhelmed to visit before. You could be thinking about asking for a promotion or a raise or about looking for a new job. And you may also find yourself standing up to people who may have intimidated you in the past. These are all signs of inner strength and waning shyness.

- You are ready to make some big changes in your living situation. You may want to redecorate, remodel, or even move. If you've been associating your surroundings with feeling bad, wanting to change them is a way of telling yourself that you are ready to feel good again. Start small: try moving some furniture around or taking a trip before you put the house on the market.

- You are able to take your disappointments in stride. Incidents that would have upset you before and sent you into a tailspin feel like only minor inconveniences now. This is a a very clear sign that you are healing from within. Whenever you can take disappointment in stride, you are robbing your negative emotions of their power, which allows you to put your emotional energy to better use.

- You understand that bad days are only temporary. We all have bad days, but for someone who has been battling shyness, they can be overwhelming. If you know that you are coming out of a difficult place, despite momentary setbacks, it's a good sign that you're developing resilience.

- You have more moments of peace and you are sleeping better. Both are signs that your mood is on the mend. You may not recognize those peaceful moments right away, but if you've been used to waking up with anxiety, and you are doing this less often, you are moving in the right direction.

- If you take a medication for anxiety or depression, you may start forgetting to take it. (This is not recommended.) When you begin to feel better, you naturally gravitate away from your prescriptions. If you find yourself forgetting more than just a few times, you need to consult with your physician. It may be time to change your dose or start tapering off. Never quit a medication without notifying your doctor and therapist.

As you continue to heal you will also grow as a person, and your relationships will deepen. It's all too easy to get used to being shy. Don't let that happen to you. Hold fast to the positive events and changes you observe as you become more empowered.

43.

How to Say No When You're Shy

Saying no is hard for the average person. It can be downright frightening for a shy person. You may be afraid to say no for a number of reasons. You may feel that you're letting the other person down. You may even fear that you're risking a friendship, simply by saying no. Another big fear is having to ask others for a favor, even when you really need one.

If you have ever agreed to something because you were too shy to say no, you probably started to feel anxious immediately. If you practice standing up for yourself and saying no, it can help you avoid the resentment, anxiety, and sticky situations that result from a lack of boundaries. A couple I knew bought their dream home together, but within a year found themselves living on the edge, full of stress and anxiety about whether they'd be able to make their payments on time every month. Being aware of your ability to follow through on an agreement can be as useful as just saying no. Remember that you always have choices.

Many people avoid saying no simply because they don't want to hurt another person's feelings. Sometimes this can be a cultural thing. During my first visit to Turkey, I attended a dinner party. I had been advised beforehand that if I was offered more food than I could eat, I should not decline, but say thank you instead. The word *no* has negative connotations, especially when your host has spent hours cooking for you. A more graceful way to say no is "I'm sorry." For example, if someone asks you for a big or inappropriate favor—if, say, your friend has decided to buy a new car but needs to borrow several thousand dollars from you until the next paycheck comes—you can say, "I'm sorry, but I don't think I can help you."

In the workplace, there are many "softer" ways of saying no that feel more like saying yes. Here are two: "Not right now" and "May I get back to you?" Some people always seem to in the throes of an urgent matter that isn't really an emergency. Saying yes to a project that is more than you can handle can be a crucial mistake with serious negative consequences. If you are overwhelmed with requests, instead of saying no, try saying "I'll have someone get back to you." This way, you can maintain your position without completely abandoning the person's request. These kinds of responses are best for shy people who have a really hard time saying no and who don't have a lot of practice with it.

Exercise

Think back on a time when you were too shy or scared to say no. You probably said yes because you were caught off guard and didn't have time to think through a response. Now, think about what you could have said instead. Brainstorm several options, and imagine the person's response to each and how it would make you feel. Sometimes having "talking points" at the ready can be a boon for really shy people, because they can rely on these go-to, stock phrases without having to scramble awkwardly for an answer. See if it doesn't help you the next time you want to say no.

Shy people can easily fall victim to people who take a yard when they are given an inch. For this reason, being able to say no in a variety of situations is a useful and necessary skill. As you become better at this skill, you'll find that it diminishes your anxiety rather than increasing it.

44.

Independence

There are some people who appear shy around other people but see themselves quite differently. They are able to reframe their preferences for dealing with the world; instead of seeing shyness, they see independence, and this is very empowering. Here are a few questions to ask yourself, to help you determine whether you might be more independent than you think:

1. Do you go to the movies, out to eat, or to events alone?

2. Do you have solo hobbies that keep you entertained?

3. Do you support a cause and express your opinion about it to others?

4. Do you live alone (or want to)?

5. Do you prefer to play individual sports over team sports?

If you answered yes to three or more of these questions, you have a strong independent streak inside of you, and it needs to be celebrated and nurtured.

There are many people with varying degrees of shyness who have made great changes in their own lives and in the world. Many you've likely never heard of, because they prefer to keep a low profile, even if they are famous in their respective fields. Shyness does not have to keep you from making your life and the lives of others better. You picked up this book for a reason—you want to be more involved with people and the world—so it makes sense to discover and learn to trust your independence.

Being independent doesn't mean that you don't need or like other people. It means that if you want to do something, you don't need someone else there to do it with you. This

isn't shyness; it is a desire to express yourself and be an individual. Yes, you may feel a little nervous when it comes to
being social, but is it your shyness that is stopping you, or is
it a lack of faith in your own ability or likeability? Self-doubt
is a big contributor to shyness and it is something that you
need to look at and work through to make life what you want
it to be. Trusting that you have what it takes is all that is
necessary to embrace and use your independence. You will
broaden your horizons by letting that independent person
out into the world.

Exercise

For a shy person to claim and embrace her independence, it has to first be discovered and integrated
into the self. Look hard at your life and make a list of
the things you have done independently. Then make
another list of the things you haven't done because
of your shyness. Compare the two lists. What you
will see is that there have been times when you were
feeling shy, but made the choice to overcome your
fear and go forward with what you wanted to do anyway. You will also see those times when your shyness
stopped you, but in retrospect it's obvious to you that
pushing through the shyness would have worked out
okay: you would have gotten through it and maybe
even enjoyed yourself. Focus on those times when
you made the decision to "feel the fear and do it anyway." Celebrate that feisty, independent side of you.
Nurture it, and it will grow.

Reframing your shyness as independence will help you see that you have a great deal more spirit and chutzpah than you may have thought. Once you take hold of this, it will make being you much easier and a lot more fun!

45.

Introverts vs. Extraverts

Research has shown that introverts are naturally anxious; when they are exposed to excess stimuli, such as large crowds of people, it tends to increase their anxiety. Extraverts are, of course, the opposite of introverts; they actually need all those stimuli to get energized and involved in activities. They also tend to be more assertive and to enjoy big gatherings such as parties. Introverts tend to be shy and to get their energy by being alone, whereas extraverts tend to get their energy from being with others and exploring the world outside the self. If you are an introvert, the thought of going to a party probably makes your palms a bit sweaty.

Some of this may have to do with how you attached with your parents and family of origin when you were little. Attachment theorists claim that children with low self-worth and low competence are more likely to have insecure attachments. Conversely, children with secure attachments are comfortable making new friends and interacting with others in new situations. If you're an introvert, it doesn't mean you're doomed, though. Not by any means! One thing that many introverts are not aware of is how much control they really have over others' perceptions of them in social settings.

If you are an introvert and parties make you anxious, there are many things you can do to reduce your anxiety. For example, Martha felt very anxious at parties where she didn't know anyone, when she didn't know what to expect, or when she wasn't familiar with the location. She was afraid of showing up to a party in a suit and seeing everyone else wearing casual clothes. She discovered that gathering as many details about the party as she could beforehand alleviated a lot of her anxiety and enabled her to prepare in advance.

Exercise

Try to participate in some social activities, even if doing so creates a lot of discomfort for you. Look for events that are affordable and ask friend to join you. You can find many such activities on local Websites. You can also look up your local chamber of commerce for network meetings in your area. Volunteering can help boost your confidence, as well. Focusing on a task will help you feel less anxious about socializing. Sometimes you can even attend an event for free if you volunteer your time for part of it. Another great place for introverts is the local farmer's market: you will run into neighbors and also get a chance to chat

with strangers while sampling all the delicious offer-
ings. And don't forget your local library: they often
host lectures, movie showings, and book clubs that
are free to the public.

46.

Is It Social Anxiety Disorder?

Shyness involves feelings of discomfort and embarrassment around people, and anxiety regarding social situations, especially those that involve strangers. Some shy folks
have to deal with a double whammy: they also suffer from
social anxiety disorder (SAD), a social phobia and anxiety
disorder that is common among adults. While people with
social phobia tend to dislike social gatherings for obvious
reasons, many would love to be involved in social gatherings
but instead always seem to find themselves on the sidelines
as observers. If you find yourself unable to carry out many of
your daily activities due to intense shyness or fear of social
interactions, you may suffer from SAD.

One of the best things you can do is tell yourself that
something positive will come from socializing with new people. Remind yourself that shy people can maintain satisfy-
ing relationships using the social skills they have developed.

Try attending different events. If you are worried about not having the right attire, look through fashion magazines in bookstores or online and zoom in on a few outfits that would help you fit in. When it comes to meeting new people, think about the kinds of relationships *you* would like to have, and then connect with people who fit those desires. If you are at a large party, look for people who seem similar to you and who interest you in some way.

Exercise

In order to get used to talking with others, start small by calling restaurants to make reservations. Ask the host or hostess questions such as "What is your specialty?" or "Which day is your busiest?" Make phone calls to follow up on your car insurance policy and your credit cards, or call to check on your airline miles account. Call your bank or your credit card company to find out how you can earn some percentage back on your purchases. These baby steps will help you build confidence in a safe environment.

47.

Know Thyself

Knowing yourself is the beginning of all wisdom.

—Aristotle

Freud was one of the first authors to explore unconscious thinking. He began analyzing dreams in order to understand the hidden aspects of the personality, and he interpreted dreams as the results of our conscious mind trying to understand the unconscious. Knowing yourself doesn't have to be this difficult or this mysterious. If you are shy, you are likely afraid to know yourself. Don't be! Get to know yourself by finding your strengths. You can find your strengths by noting and building on skills you already have, such as cooking, art, writing, or music.

Your hobbies will tell you a lot about who you are, too. Shy people tend to avoid hobbies because they are afraid of failing. You may be too shy to explore many of the hobbies that interest you because you are worried about exposing yourself to scrutiny, criticism, or failure. If you've always wanted to build model trains, for example, start working on a model on the weekends. If you've ever wanted to know how to crochet, take a course at your local community center and start making little knitted gifts for your friends and family members. Remind yourself that your fear of failure can only prevent you from following your dreams and goals.

You are the only person who can tell you that you can't do something!

When you know yourself, you will be at greater peace with yourself, with others, and with life in general.

48.

Know When to Stand Up for Yourself

When you're shy, it can be very hard to stand up for yourself when you are wrongly accused or challenged in a confrontational way. Most shy people stay as far away from confrontation as possible, but unfortunately it is a part of life and cannot be avoided completely. As a shy person, learning to stand up for yourself and face confrontation head-on may be the most important thing you can do to keep your life moving in a positive direction.

Being bullied or threatened is traumatic and difficult for anyone, but for a shy person it is pure misery. Even if you've done nothing wrong, someone who knows your trigger points can use them against you as leverage. This is enough to make anyone want to run away! Maybe you decide to take the blame and give the aggressor whatever it is he wants, in hopes that it will make that person go away. Once a bully knows that he can get one over on you, however, he won't stop. You must learn to protect yourself in these situations. Walking away is one way to do that, and sometimes it's the right thing to do. However, other techniques can be more beneficial, depending on the context.

Preparing yourself for these situations ahead of time is probably the single best thing you can do. It will help you find strength and will assist in further reducing your shyness factor. Start out by looking at how you typically react when you are confronted, your default reaction. Everyone is different in this regard. For example, when your teenager asks you for money to get their nose pierced and you say "no" expect a little attitude, that's normal. What you need to do is to correct your child and tell the kid it isn't okay for them to speak to you that way, and close the conversation by telling them you love them—and their nose.

When the confrontation comes from an adult, perhaps a coworker or even someone you thought was a friend, you need to deal with it a little differently. First ask the person if she would be willing to have a two-way conversation about the issue. If she says no, then you need to respond by saying something along the lines of "Okay, when you are ready to talk about it, I am open, but I won't be verbally assaulted [or demeaned, or shamed, or whatever the violation was] by anyone." I know these are strong words, and they may be scary to say (especially if the other person has more power or is bigger than you), but you cannot allow yourself to be abused for any reason; it is a violation, pure and simple, and it opens the door for more of the same.

Once the other person is calm enough to discuss the problem, then you can begin to correct any misunderstandings or miscommunications. Be grown-up enough to admit if you have made a mistake or contributed to the problem in some way, but do not allow blame to "land" when there is none. What's important here is that you don't let your shyness put you in the position to be emotionally injured repeatedly. The first time that someone abuses you should always be the last.

There is a lot to think about, here. Most of the practice for this kind of thing has to take place in your own head. Think long and hard, because no one has the right to make you cower, and if you are in the right, you should be proud of it.

49.

Learn to Strike Up a Conversation

One of life's best gifts is a good conversation. It costs you nothing, you enjoy the process, and you are left with positive feelings and a desire to learn more about the other person, and sometimes the topic at hand, a little bit better. An enjoyable verbal exchange can inspire you and boost your energy.

Sometimes the most awkward part of a conversation is getting it started. Striking up a conversation can be scary for shy people, even when it's with someone they are already acquainted with, let alone when it's with a complete stranger. For the painfully shy, doing the latter can feel like an impossible proposition. One of my mentors, the late Dr. Albert Ellis, was a very shy man who wanted to get past it. So he did an experiment back in the 1960s, one that probably would have gotten him arrested if he tried it today. He sat on a bench in New York's Central Park and asked *every single woman* who passed by out for coffee. Terrifying, right? The experiment was a failure in the sense that only one woman said yes, and she didn't even show up for the date. However, he definitely got over his fear of asking someone out! He also created cognitive behavioral therapy, wrote 72 books, and was still doing weekly lectures at the age of 90. Obviously, he did not let his shyness hold him back, and he taught himself to converse not only with strange women but also with large groups of colleagues. It is hard for sensitive and shy people to understand that they can get past their fears by facing them. But it is one of the many exercises that work. If you'd like to get better at striking up a conversation, as Dr. Ellis did, there are countless ways to do it. Making it a goal is the first step.

Exercise

Try going to a local chamber of commerce meeting. Shake as many hands as possible as you exchange names, professions, and business cards. The networking part may be helpful in other ways, but the idea is to get comfortable talking with people you've never met before. If you can do it in one environment, you can do it in another. The nice thing about a business setting is that you have ready-made conversation starters, because everyone is already talking about what they do for a living. For some people, a strictly social situation creates much more anxiety.

If you need to start more slowly, attend a religious service or check out a social or cultural group that interests you. Such venues tend to be more welcoming than strictly professional meetings. Many organizations have designated greeters to make newcomers feel more comfortable.

These are just a few examples of actions you can take to help you become more comfortable at striking up a conversation. Before you know it, you'll be asking people out on a park bench!

50.

Live a Full Life

The Egyptian word *aish* means "bread," but it also means "to live." It is amazing and powerful how this one word can have two important and interconnected meanings. For Egytians, to eat bread *is* to live. What does life mean to you?

We sometimes limit ourselves to living one life, or even half a life, while we dream of an impossible ideal—of speaking new languages, of being a teacher or bank teller or skydiver, of playing a musical instrument in a band. It might seem impossible for a shy person to live a full life, let alone several lives. But why not live as many lives as you can by finding the time to do all of the things that you desire?

Shy people often stick to a basic routine or a rote lifestyle because of their fears. When I say, "Don't allow your shyness to limit you to living just one life," I mean that you should imagine yourself as someone who can have multiple qualities, interests, personality traits, occupations, strengths, and skills. For example, when you get home from work or school, you probably just want stare at the TV until you fall asleep. When you get home tomorrow, practice a new recipe instead. (If you ask how this can help your shyness, learning to cook new dishes is always useful during get-togethers and holiday parties.) Likewise, if you have ever taken music or language lessons, practice what you've learned for 20 minutes every time you get home. Many teachers will tell you that it only takes this small time investment to enhance your skills and increase your ability to retain them.

Each new experience that we have in life is unique. If you expect to have the same experiences with different people and circumstances, you are limiting your enjoyment of what is truly new. Along with embracing the new, we must still put down good roots for growth and security, however. Think of a tree. If that tree is uprooted and moved to a new location every few months, it will never thrive. This concept is the same in our lives. We must create stability in our lives in order to be able to flourish. That stability will come when you take responsibility for your own happiness and work toward being able to live the type of life—or lives—that you most desire. *Don't allow your shyness to limit your ability to truly live.*

51.

Listening Skills for the Shy at Heart

Shyness can really get in the way of being a good listener. This is because it's hard to focus on others when you are focused on your own social anxiety. Fortunately being a good listener involves several learned skills and behaviors. These include receiving a message; attending to it by a gesture, such as a head nod; interpreting that message; and showing that you have understood the message by rephrasing, restating, asking a question, or some other method. Mainly, effective listening requires giving an active response. This means it takes some effort and doesn't just happen on its own.

Some other important listening skills include tuning in, maintaining open body language, and asking questions only after the other person has finished talking. Some bad listening habits include interrupting, presenting defensive body language or posture, making assumptions, losing focus or looking away, worrying about what you are going to say, and only listening selectively to what you want to hear. Interrupting others is just rude, and if you are busy worrying about what you want to say, you may not remember what the speaker has said.

Shy people often appear not to be listening because they tend to do things that are misinterpreted, such as looking away or down at the floor. If you are shy, make a point of maintaining eye contact with the other person. It may feel awkward and artificial at first, but studies have shown that eye contact has a positive relationship with listening. The better the eye contact you have, the more likely you are to listen. Remember that it is normal to glance away once in a while, but not for an extended period of time.

If you're just not interested in the topic at hand, or you're not in the mood to talk, your listening skills may decline even further. It's also easy to tune someone out when you already know a lot about the subject. Even if you feel you know everything about, say, coffee, that isn't a reason to shut out someone who wants to share her own coffee experience or brewing tips with you.

Exercise

Practice your listening skills. Learn different ways to provide an empathetic response, such as "I'm sorry to hear that," when a friend or colleague shares bad news. If you have a hard time listening for long periods of time, you can practice by listening to radio shows or prerecorded lectures. Other useful techniques include giving feedback, accepting feedback, and visualization. Another great technique is to put yourself in the speaker's shoes and imagining how you would feel if someone were responding to you in the same way.

You will probably have to do your most active listening at work, so it's imperative to remember to listen actively at work. Important listening habits at work include taking turns and avoiding distractions. Even if you disagree with something, allow the other person to finish without interrupting him or her. Make sure ahead of time that your phone won't go off, and avoid daydreaming or staring out the window during a conversation, regardless of how casual the setting is.

As a shy person, you'll probably have to make an extra effort to show people that you are listening. It's worth it, though: these skills can help you get past your shyness, and other people will only appreciate feeling heard. Win-win!

52.

Listen to Your Heart

One of the best ways to overcome your shyness is to learn to listen to your heart. It may sound a little corny, but most of the time we are so caught up in what's going on in our heads that we forget about our emotional selves. If your heart isn't in it, not much is going to happen.

If this is something that is new for you, a great way to start is by simply placing your hand on your heart. Just being able to feel your pulse and heartbeat is a wonderful way to get in touch with that wonderful organ, the one that is strong enough to overcome even the worst case of shyness you have ever had. By feeling your heart, you actually sync your brain with the rhythm of its beat; in this way, you will be better able to understand the messages that are coming from your emotional self.

Often, however, it's your brain that's the one in charge, sending information to your heart based on your proclivity toward shyness. The habit of being a shy person—and yes, it is in many ways a habit—may be so ingrained that it is next to impossible to override those messages. Attending to the truth that your heart is telling you can help you vanquish your shyness and enable you to enjoy life in ways you never could have imagined.

Exercise

Write down what you think your brain is saying and what you feel your heart is saying in two separate columns. Do the two match up? If not, which one do you want to follow? By choosing to follow your heart, you are giving yourself the advantage of the strength that comes from all the love you've ever received. Once you feel it, that love can overpower your shyness, and your heart's desire to be with other people will no longer scare you.

If you approach others with an open heart, they will feel it (if they have any sensitivity at all) and will most likely return a similar energy to you. That's how great relationships are born, one open heart reaching out to and touching another. It's what we all want, and it is available to you by just being willing to listen to your heart.

53.

Listen to Your Intuition

Intuition can give us a lot of good information and provide us with the inspiration we need to overcome our shyness. Many times our anxiety, the fears in our head, speaks so loudly that we can't hear the recommendations of our gut, which always has our best interests at heart. When you get a gut feeling, listen to it.

It's sometimes difficult to distinguish between intuitive messages and those that come from fear. An easy way to tell them apart is by meditating. I remember sitting in a doctor's office because I had been in mourning for the loss of my love from cancer and had been giving myself a bunch of psychosomatic symptoms. There were a lot of very sick people in the waiting room. It was so crowded I had to sit on the floor! I looked around and closed my eyes to meditate for a moment, to see if I could get in touch with what was really going on inside me. What I heard in my head was that I was not nearly as sick as everyone else in the room, and that what I *should* do was heal my emotional pain; the physical stuff would take care of itself. The doctor said just about the same thing to me.

Here's another example. Let's say you're at a party and you spot someone you'd really like to talk to. Your first reaction will, of course, be driven by shyness, and you might hear a great big *no* resounding in your head. Take a moment, put your hand on your heart, and feel what the intuitive part of your being is saying to you instead. Intuition doesn't lie, but it can be difficult to hear when your shyness is in full gear, so take your time and wait for the right answer. You may be surprised at what you hear.

These are just two examples of how getting in touch with your intuition can help you uncover and deal with a problem. Whatever or whoever put this insecurity inside of you can be found and healed, simply by taking the time to go inside your own mind and looking at who you are at the moment, and who you can be in the future. Your intuition will always let you know whether a certain action is safe. Remember: it always has your best interests at heart.

Your intuition can guide you in many ways. Listen to that part of yourself and let it make you stronger than your shyness. You already are.

54.

Loneliness and Shyness

Shy people tend to like being alone. Just because you're alone doesn't mean that you're lonely. Sometimes you need to be alone, in order to understand yourself, to know what you want, to decompress, or to decide what will make you happy. However, you don't want to condition yourself to being alone, especially if you are secretly longing for human interaction.

Loneliness is both an emotional and a psychological experience. When we experience loneliness long enough, we are more likely to experience depression and anxiety. Loneliness can affect our mood and social skills. It can also impair the immune system and increase inflammation, making us vulnerable to all kinds of illnesses and diseases, such as type II diabetes, arthritis, and heart disease. I once had a patient who would rather sit alone in his apartment than be surrounded by people at a nursing home. The idea of going to a nursing home upset him, understandably, and he claimed that he liked being alone well enough. But then he contradicted himself and said that he was lonely.

Shyness and loneliness develop as early as elementary school, and they tend to go together. Women are more likely to report feeling lonely, although more men suffer from shyness than women. If you are shy, you can reduce your loneliness by participating in activities with others. Even something as simple as making a commitment to meet with a friend at least once a week can help decrease the thoughts that contribute to feeling lonely.

Finally, get in touch with your feelings when you are alone; if you feel uncomfortable or isolated, challenge yourself by joining a local meet-up group. If you want to start enjoying your time alone—and we all need that downtime from time to time—try a solo activity, such as hiking or going for walks.

55.

Make More Friends

The energy you get from people who care about you is a gift. People who enjoy close relationships and friendships generally live longer and fuller lives. We need to realize how much we need each other to get along in this world. I believe that we are meant to interact and have relationships with one another; if not, why are there so many people on the planet? We are not meant to be alone, though there will always be misanthropes (those who don't like other people). The desire to have a special someone to bond with is human nature and deeply rooted in our DNA. When we long for contact and don't have any, it can make for a very depressing life. The problem is, for shy people, making new friends can be scary. So how do you do this?

They say the best way to make a friend is to be one, and I agree. When you do nice things for nice people, everyone feels good, and trust begins to develop. Most friendships start off slowly and grow over time. I am suspicious of any relationship that fires up too quickly, as such relationships tend to burn out just as quickly. Work can be a great place to start. Spending time with people from the office is an easy, often nonthreatening way to find someone to hang out with. Most people want to grab a bite or have a drink after their day is done. It's also easier to make conversation in this context, because you already have work in common.

You get to know people by asking questions and sharing information about your life. Whom have you told your story to? What do you want to know about your coworkers? Conversations have to have a topic, and there is plenty happening in the world these days to talk about. Being in agreement isn't necessary. In fact, not being of the same opinion can make for a much more interesting conversation; just don't put the other person down or write him off just because he has a different outlook.

To be a good friend and to make equally good friends, remain true to your values and extend yourself if someone you know is in need. Just answering a simple question or helping someone with a menial task can jump-start a conversation and a friendship. But you have to put yourself out there a little, so the next time you see someone you'd like to get to know better, look for an opportunity to lend a hand or share something meaningful. The results will be beneficial to both of you.

By pushing past your shyness and investing in others, you will make more friends and develop great relationships.

56.

Meetings

Overcoming shyness in the business world can be difficult because there is so much on the line. No one is immune from encountering difficulties at work, and nowhere is this more applicable than in meetings. But meetings don't have to be an awful experience, even if you're shy.

Think of ways to make the meetings you run or attend more pleasant. You can start by arriving early and choosing a good seat. Try to think positively and be enthusiastic during the meeting. Make valuable suggestions and offer solutions to problems instead of hanging back as an observer or, worse, only offering criticisms. If you sit in the back of meetings to avoid being called on, this might backfire and end up bringing more attention to you. So instead of hiding and hoping for the meeting to end quickly, become involved in the discussion and in preparing materials, such as handouts, ahead of time. Being involved in running the meeting can help you let down your defenses.

If you have to make a presentation, the most difficult part might be the discussion that comes afterward. Having to field questions and even criticism can be pure agony for a shy person. Take a deep breath and keep some water handy. When the discussion starts, don't compete with other group members. Listen to everyone, and take notes to show your interest in each person's ideas. Don't let your shyness keep you from expressing your thoughts and feelings. Look for consensus, and try to agree on decisions as a group rather than making them unilaterally.

Being unprepared for this part of the meeting will only make you more anxious. You can prepare by writing down some questions you are likely to hear, and brainstorming several possible answers to each. Be open to questioning in both your words and your body language. This will make it a more pleasant experience for everyone.

Finally, know that everyone gets nervous in these situations. You just may have to do a little more preparing on the front end to give yourself an advantage over your shyness.

57.

Move Your Body

Shyness can lead to a sedentary lifestyle. If you don't go out much and you want to avoid people, going to a gym isn't going to be all that appealing to you. Even going outside for a jog can be intimidating if you think you're going to run into other people or if you feel as though you're on display. If you don't move around, though, you're actually depriving your body of the energy it needs to function properly. Getting your body moving is also one of the best antianxiety and antidepressants available, and it's free. So what can you do as a shy person to be more active?

You don't have to become a gym rat to get the exercise you need. Dance, get up and walk around the room, pick up your clothes, clean the house, or work out to a YouTube video. Cleaning out the garage, doing yard work, and even walking the dog will help you feel better. Once you get those endorphins circulating through your brain, you can't help but feel more energy. Embracing a more physical lifestyle will make you feel more optimistic about almost everything; doing it to music will make it that much more enjoyable.

If you really can't find anything at home you'd like to do, that could actually be a good thing because it will basically force you to get out. I am lucky enough to live in a walking destination zone. People drive to my area so they can get some exercise and look at the scenery as they do it. The days I take that walk are always better than the days I feel too lazy to go out. It's been a great way to meet lots of people, most of whom I don't know except by their dogs' names, but there's nothing wrong with that.

A friend of mine whose husband passed away late in life was struggling with what to do with her time. A breast cancer survivor herself, she considered just letting life pass her by and waiting for her time. Well, her plan wasn't meant to be, because her children gave her a cell phone and a Yorkie; she knew that if she didn't take that little dog out, it would make a mess in her home. So she started walking him every day. Then she met a few people and joined the yacht club. As of this writing, she's there a few times a week, and at 90 years old she can still dance the night away.

Getting your body moving will help you overcome your shyness. Now put on some music and dance like nobody's watching.

58.

No Pain, No Gain

❝No pain, no gain" is an exercise motto that promises greater rewards at the cost of hard, even painful work. This actually applies to emotional pain, as well. According to neuroscientists, the brain responds to social rejection in the same way it responds to physical pain. Rejection hurts so badly because the same chemicals that are released into our brains when feel physical pain are released when we are rejected. Fortunately, our brains also release natural painkillers—opioids—that help us manage and rebound from both physical and emotional pain. Shy people tend to experience more social rejection, which means that it is important for them to learn to build up their natural resilience to pain. As you learn to adjust to setbacks, this leads to a higher degree of natural painkiller activation, and greater resilience in the face of social rejection.

If you have ever avoided a job interview or a date out of shyness, ask yourself what emotions you felt when you were hurt in the past, and why. When we hang onto negative events from our past, we prevent ourselves from excelling in the future. How you respond to rejection determines your future success. If you are shy, rejection may have caused you to feel embarrassment or shame, which may have resulted in a desire to isolate and avoid further pain. Don't blame yourself for being rejected. Come to terms with it, and remember that there is *always* some gain with the pain. The gain is learning to endure, regardless of the outcome. Resilience in the face of rejection will help you flourish. If you allow yourself to remain stuck in the hurt phase, you won't be able to reap the rewards that come from facing and moving through, not around, your pain.

When you are adjusting to a new relationship, environment, or schedule, the first thirty days are the most difficult. Remind yourself to take it easy, as full adjustment can take up to six months. Do things that make you feel good and remind you of good times. This can be something as simple as going to your favorite restaurant or watching an old black-and-white movie. Encourage yourself to engage in social activities more often. This will activate your reward system by increasing the activity of your opioid receptors. Most of us want to avoid pain. However, if we fear rejection to the point that our fear hinders our social life, then we are only opening the door to an unhealthy lifestyle of isolation and low moods, such as sadness and depression.

Exercise

Self-handicapping, negative thoughts—for example, thinking *I will always fail*—will probably increase when you are under some type of threat. Offset this by repeating positive self-affirmations while getting dressed or just before a social event, affirmations such as *I am wonderful* or *I look great*. Remember that working on your inner self may require some deep soul searching and may bring to mind past pain. In the end, however, you will reap the reward.

Your aim through all of this should be to push through the temporary pain—the anxiety, the fear, the discomfort—and learn to increase your comfort around others. This will only serve to increase your self-esteem and reduce your shyness. Your gain will be in being able to tolerate and even enjoy social activities.

59.

Nonverbal Communication

There are many ways to communicate that do not involve speaking, such as gestures, posture, and facial expressions. Shy people often avoid communicating through eye contact and facial expressions, as well as through physical touch. However, the good thing about nonverbal forms of communication is that they can be easier to practice. For example, try using facial expressions such as nods and smiles to send positive messages to others. Facial expressions have the same meanings across many if not most cultures. A smile in the United States means the same thing that it does in Taiwan, Dusseldorf, and Moscow. Such expression have been hardwired into our genes, allowing us to understand and conncct with total strangers without saying a word.

Nonverbal communication can also include posture and gestures. Uncrossing your limbs can indicate openness and agreement; leaning forward shows that you're trying to understand the other person; and eye contact and physical contact, such as shaking hands, indicate a desire to connect. Shy people become uncomfortable in social settings easily, and may unconsciously step backward to create a bigger space between themselves and others. Try to avoid these and other nonverbal behaviors that suggest nervousness or standoffishness, such as wiggling or fidgeting in your chair, clearing your throat, tugging at your ear, playing with your hair, or staring at the floor while you speak. If someone is unaware of your shyness, these behaviors can send confusing signals that you are disinterested in or dismissive of the person or the topic. Perhaps not surprisingly, shy people tend to use fewer facial expressions in general when speaking.

Exercise

Practice your positive, nonverbal skills when you are alone at home. Keep your arms and legs uncrossed while watching television; when you're brushing your teeth, make eye contact with yourself in the mirror. It may feel weird at first, but the idea is to train yourself and make the behaviors habitual. Another great way to build your nonverbal communication skills is to take a dance class, because so much of dance, especially when done with a partner, involves communicating nonverbally.

The majority of what we say is expressed through nonverbal cues, so learning positive ways to communicate nonverbally will only contribute to improving your communication skills and, hence, reducing your shyness. Remember, practice makes perfect.

60.

Nurture Your Self-Respect

Self-respect is a necessary prerequisite for participating fully in the world and fulfilling your dreams, but both will be insurmountable hurdles if you don't feel you deserve such things to begin with. Without self-respect, it will be difficult if not impossible for you to get past your shyness.

A lack of self-respect can manifest in many ways; extreme shyness is one of the major ones. How can you deal with other people and the world if you don't feel you are *respect-able*—able or deserving of being respected? You need to respect yourself first if you expect others to be able to do so. Being unable to respect yourself is a sign that you may need some inner healing. To this end, it's important to take a look at your internal dialogue, because your brain is likely telling you things that may not be true about yourself.

Ask yourself what it is about you that you don't respect. Where did all those negative thoughts come from? Are they really your thoughts? Perhaps that inner critic was planted there by a harsh parent or guardian when you were a child; perhaps a professional or personal relationship that went south later on only served to amplify this feeling. Whatever the case may be, you need to discover the origin or root cause of your lack of self-respect. Finding out where things started is paramount in being able to heal the issues and hurts that hold you back.

A lack of self-respect can also come from living in the shadow of greatness. If your parents were/are famous or influential people, it can make you question how much you can really contribute, and that will only increase your reticence and shyness. Many of us have worked for people that have accomplished great things, but could they have done it without the help of others? Even if you feel you have failed over and over in life, you still possess talents and abilities, gifts that you need to recognize and tap into. Nobody is inadequate at everything: there are things you are good at but maybe just haven't discovered yet.

If you lack true self-respect, you will always want to hide. You won't be empowered to reach for the stars or even just go to Starbucks. You may think that self-medication with drugs or alcohol is the answer, because sometimes they provide a temporary feeling of relief and personal power, but know that this is a lie. True self-worth comes from within, not from a bottle of booze or pills. There is no way around it: you'll have to do this from the inside out, even though you may be looking at outside accomplishments (yours and those of others) to gauge your internal feelings about yourself.

Exercise

Honestly look at the person you are and make a list of what is *good* about you. Take your time, a few days at least, and keep on adding to it. Ask others—friends, colleagues, family—for their input, because sometimes it's hard to see yourself objectively. Now here's the really important part: look at this entire list every day. Memorize it. To the degree that you make it a part of your psyche, that's how much it will reinforce your self-respect and give you an emotional boost that will help you overcome your shyness.

Once you do the hard work, life will improve in so many ways. When the penny finally drops, you will wonder why you ever doubted yourself. You'll even be able to make up for all the time you lost to that inner critic, because your energy will skyrocket. All from learning how to respect yourself.

61.

Nurture the Trust in Your Relationships

Living with the strength of spirit you get from knowing that someone you love and trust has your back is such an amazing shyness eraser! It's one of the most wonderful parts of being connected to another person and a great reason for being in a relationship. Unfortunately, being shy can make it hard to trust other people. In fact, your shyness may have been caused in part by someone you cared for (or thought cared for you) but who broke trust with you in some way. As the saying goes, once bitten, twice shy. Although it's difficult to think about, knowing how your shyness started or what contributed to it along the way will make it easier to overcome.

Don't disrespect the trust that is given to you, but honor it by stepping up when you are called upon or needed. Typically when there is a crisis, I can come forward and do my part; it's only afterward that I feel the fear. We all have different ways of dealing with difficulties, but when someone I care about is in trouble, all of my shyness seems to go away, and I am there for that person no matter what.

When someone you trust asks for your help or just your company, what's the first thing that comes to mind? Do you let your fears overshadow your care and concern? Yes, you may feel some anxiety here, at first. But if you don't let it take over your thinking, and hold the emotion at bay, your stronger self—the self that both trusts and is trustworthy—will have the opportunity to show up. It's always right there, but your shyness doesn't let you see it readily sometimes.

Building trust with another human being is something that happens over time, especially for a shy person. When a relationship characterized by trust is firmly in place, however, it becomes infinitely more powerful than your shyness. Think about that. Through the love, your shyness is minimized and even vanquished altogether. What a wonderful way to let go of what holds you back!

Perhaps the biggest part of nurturing trust is being a trustworthy person, and not betraying that trust. Ever. When someone else puts his or her trust in you, it is something sacred. I feel this often in my therapy practice, but less so in real life. It is hard to trust, and I think it gets harder with time because you have experienced more broken promises and betrayal. But once you let it in and return it in kind, your ability to enjoy and experience life grows.

Have you broken trust with someone? Now is the time to rebuild what may have been lost in an important relationship. Talk with that person and get the healing process started. You need to be able to trust the people you love *and* feel their trust in you. Having that in your heart and head will help you overcome your shyness in ways that nothing else can.

Allowing yourself to trust a new person may be a little more challenging, but, again, the secret to making it work is to be trustworthy yourself. If you care for someone and want to be closer to that person, show him or her that you deserve trust by being the kind of person who can always be counted upon—a trustworthy person. It will change both your lives.

62.

OCD and Shyness

The term OCD, which stands for obsessive-compulsive disorder, is thrown around a lot these days. Some people even use it as a badge of honor: "Oh, I'm so OCD, you should see how neat and clean my house/desk/child is!" Many of my clients believe that they have obsessive-compulsive disorder, or OCD. One in particular, who used to be very social and engaging at events and family get-togethers, is now beset by fears as soon as she leaves her house. Her fears range from coming in contact with other people and catching colds, to avoiding public restrooms out of a fear of germs. Now she tries to stay home as much as possible.

OCD is a very specific condition and can only be properly diagnosed if it is taking up at least an hour of your time every day and interferes with your ability to function socially. People with OCD sometimes engage in repetitive activities, such as hand-washing; they feel compelled to perform them to the point that they are unable to function or hold a job. Symptoms like this can be alienating and time-consuming, and they frequently result in severe emotional and economic losses. Cognitive behavioral therapy (CBT) accompanied by antidepressant medications are two of the best interventions for true OCD.

A diagnosis of OCD can make a shy person feel even shyer. Due to fears of being found out or confronted, there's even more of a reason to avoid other people. Although they may long for social interaction and try their best to stay connected with people in order to feel alive, people who have OCD are aware of the irrationality of their own thoughts and behaviors, which frequently leads to escalation of symptoms, including isolating behaviors.

Shy people sometimes engage in behaviors that resemble those of people with OCD. For example, if people are coming over to visit, you may suddenly be motivated (out of anxiety) to clean your home obsessively. If you are having negative thoughts about inviting people over, immediately think of a positive reason for doing so. When friends and family members visit, they can help you break out of your shyness. You will become more comfortable around others if you can start with baby steps by hosting people on your home turf.

If you find that your obsessive behaviors are becoming more intrusive and burdensome, even a daily occurrence, talk to a therapist who is trained in such matters. While shyness may or may not be a more fixed personality trait, OCD behaviors can be managed and often eliminated with the right combination of behavioral therapy and medication.

63.

Overcome Shyness With Positive Thinking

Keeping your thoughts moving in a positive direction not only makes you feel good in the moment, but it also can reduce your shyness factor measurably. It also gives you the one thing that we all need to keep our lives moving forward: hope. The more you embrace and deploy positive thinking, the longer the effects will last. The book *The Power of Positive Thinking* by Dr. Norman Vincent Peale has helped millions of people do just that. It also was one of the very first human potential/self-help books, and has served as a model for others in its genre. I strongly urge you to read it.

Even though the idea has been around a very long time and become the theme for hundreds, if not thousands, of other books, it is *not* easy to accomplish, especially if shyness has kept you from stretching yourself and stopped you from doing things you enjoy. The thing is, after living that way for a while, you actually train your mind to accept your shyness. You figure out ways to work your life around it, rather than the other way around. By employing positive thinking, however, you can change the way your thoughts control your life by taking charge of what is going on inside your head. New thoughts lead to new behaviors, which lead to new emotions, which lead to *change*.

The first thing you need to do is believe that you can do something about your condition. If you do, you are more than halfway there already! Now let's look at how you think. When it comes to socializing, it probably causes you anxiety, right? Once you have identified the problem, the next step is to think about how you would feel if things were different. Imagine walking into a room and feeling confident, your shyness only a distant memory. You are meeting and greeting people, engaging in conversations, and actually really enjoying yourself. People are flocking to you; you are so attractive and charismatic. Yes, this is just taking place in your head right now, but that's where it all starts. You have to think and imagine how you would behave *if your shyness weren't holding you back*. What would you do if you weren't afraid? Putting yourself in a new pair of psychological shoes, so to speak, is a great way of making a plan for how you will respond to new social interactions. Visualizing this kind of change in your head is incredibly powerful.

You have begun the process of changing your thinking from negative to positive. When you imagine yourself at a party, how does it make you feel? Nervous and uncomfortable? Okay, now change that thinking by saying to yourself that you will feel great at the party, and say it over and over. This is a type of affirmation that will help change your old thinking pattern and the attendant emotions that come with it.

It takes about 30 repetitions to create a new habit, so you'll need to do this exercise about 30 times to start seeing real change. The more you do it, the more positive your thinking will become, and the better you will feel. Before you know it, you will be that charismatic, witty, attractive person at the party.

64.

Perfectionism: A Cause of Shyness?

There are only two mistakes one can make along the road to truth: not going all the way, and not starting.
—Buddha

A lot of people think they can only enjoy life if it goes perfectly. Many of us make our decisions on the basis of uncertainty and the fear that we won't match someone *else's* idea of perfection. We tend to think that we need to be perfect (or at least seem perfect) in order for happiness to find us. This simply isn't true. There is not one single person on this earth who is perfect. If happiness were predicated upon perfection, then none of us would be able to be happy. Life doesn't have to be perfect for us to enjoy a moment of happiness. In fact, it could be argued that much of the beauty in ourselves, in others, and in life itself comes from the so-called imperfections—the differences, the variations—that make things interesting and joyful.

A number of studies have addressed the ways in which the different types of perfectionism (there is more than one) can result in negative social reactions. People who are very worried about how others view them also have a heightened fear of failure and rejection, and thus are more likely to have increased feelings of shame and fear of negative evaluation by others. As a result, people who feel a need for perfection may become socially withdrawn. Put more simply, perfectionism can make people shy.

Exercise

Lose some of your perfectionism by telling a few jokes and—here's the kicker—not worrying about getting a laugh. Take out a sheet of paper, write down three or four good jokes, and commit them to memory. Practice on your friends first. Try to avoid jokes that are too long; keep them short and sweet. If you're really brave, try an open-mic night at a local club. The idea is to tell the jokes and let go of the result. This can be freeing for even the most die-hard perfectionist!

Perfectionists are often easily defeated because their goals are too impossible, too lofty. If you set a goal and can't reach it, don't be excessively hard on yourself. First, set more realistic standards for your future goals, ones that you can reasonably expect to accomplish. Second, write down your goal, whether it's making new friends or getting a new job, and list the steps that are necessary to accomplish it in a reasonable time. Don't be afraid to seek moral support in the process; share your goal with friends and family members. You don't have to give anyone specific details if you don't feel comfortable. Whatever you choose to share will be one giant leap toward overcoming your shyness.

65.

Positive Actions for Reducing Shyness

I am a big believer in positive thinking. I use it, I train clients to use it, and I have written about its benefits for more than a decade. It's one of the reasons I decided to include more than one entry on it in this book. Positive thinking can help you make changes that will benefit you in so many ways. I really can't say enough good things about it. Over the years, however, I have become aware that positive thinking may not be enough to help some people overcome their shyness. The trick here is to get out of your head and start taking positive action. Rather than just keeping the positivity to yourself, you need to actually do it and, ideally, share it with others. Having a positive influence on those around you will change the way you feel inside and will naturally make you more outgoing. Just doing this can make you a happier person, even if you are dealing with a very difficult shyness issue.

Taking action means doing things that are good for you and never doing anything that could possibly harm you. For example, if you have been ill and unable to take a run or even go for a walk, you need to wait until you are well before you start exercising. What you can do in the meantime is work with a physical therapist to help you get stronger in a gradual and healthy way. The same principle holds true if you want to reduce your shyness: you don't want to try to eliminate shyness from your system overnight. Approach the process gradually and give yourself the time you need to adjust to your new healthy and balanced way of thinking about yourself.

One of the most difficult parts of dealing with shyness is our tendency to ruminate, letting the same negative thoughts keep spinning around in our brains. Getting rid of the negative thoughts by doing something fun can help to break this cycle. Getting out of the house, even if it's just to the mall, will help enormously in this regard. Not only do you get exercise by walking around, but you get to window shop, too!

Taking action also means doing what you can to keep your family and social connections strong. When you're struggling with shyness, outside observers can often see things more clearly than we can and give helpful feedback and direction. Often the people around us see things that we don't, especially when we are unhappy. It's always wise to take some time to consider the potential outcome of any advice or recommendation before taking action. There is wisdom in the counsel of many.

Doing new things actually activates positive chemicals in your brain, which makes you feel better about life and closer to your loved ones. Taking positive action makes your life better and will reduce your shyness. It's that simple—all you have to do is take the first step.

66.

Positive Self-Talk

We've already looked at positive thinking and positive actions, both of which are great techniques for people looking to overcome their shyness. Another helpful technique is positive self-talk. Affirmations are a kind of positive self-talk, and became very popular in the 1980s with the help of *Self-Healing* author and publisher Louise L. Hay, whom I had the pleasure of spending time with a couple of decades ago. Affirmations are short statements about how you are improving yourself, such as, "Every day, in every way, I am getting better and better!" This one has been around forever and there are millions more like it: "I enjoy perfect health" or "I am overcoming my shyness." The idea is that saying these statements to yourself many times throughout the day will change the way you think and feel. Yes, they work. No, you cannot just repeat affirmations to yourself and expect your life to get better. Again, you need to follow through and actually take the actions necessary to accomplish your goals.

Another way of using positive self-talk for overcoming shyness is to have a conversation with yourself about your behavior. Tell yourself that you no longer need to be shy to protect yourself, that you are safe in the world you have created. This old habit can be changed by letting yourself know that you are now in control of your life; this includes the people you choose to engage with and bring into your inner circle. You are not a victim, and you have the strength to deal with any situation, even if it causes you some anxiety.

This kind of internal dialogue will make you stronger, help alleviate your shyness, and give you more confidence. The more you do it, the better you will feel. I'm not suggesting that every thought has to be focused on overcoming your shyness, but take some time each and every day and give yourself a good talking-to. The effects are pretty quick and last as long as you continue the process, well beyond in many cases.

Exercise

First thing in the morning tomorrow, try simply saying to yourself, *Hey, I'm actually okay*, and repeat it several times until you can actually feel it somewhere in your body. This simple process can set you up for having a better day than if you had just let your negative thoughts have their way with you. See, it's not enough to just stop the negative thoughts: You have to replace them with positive thoughts and images so that you can create a stronger and more outgoing you.

If you allow yourself to continue to listen to the negativity that flashes through your brain, and you hold on to that negativity, you can make it a permanent part of your life. You are working on overcoming your shyness, so don't let yourself backslide by reinforcing negative thoughts. Instead, blast them away with your own positivity. I know you have it in you.

67.

Posture Can Help You Beat Shyness

Remember when your parents and teachers always told you to sit up straight and stand with your shoulders back and your head held high? They weren't trying to train you for the military. They probably knew that practicing good posture would have a positive effect on how you perceived yourself and how others perceived you. Believe it or not, it's also a great tool for reducing shyness. Of course good posture has health benefits, but here we're more focused on the emotional ones.

When your posture is upright and proud, you send a silent message to all those who see you that you are a confident, worthy person. You unconsciously pick up on their confidence in you, which in turn helps to build your self-esteem. It's actually an amazing process that is very real and very palpable. If you've never felt this feeling before, like most shy people, you may not realize what it is when you do.

You don't have to have an imposing physicality or be a body builder or even a dedicated gym rat to make this work for you. It isn't about being in great physical shape (though that doesn't hurt, and can actually benefit you in many other ways); it's about an outward expression that helps create an inner attitude and feeling. What we do with our bodies affects our emotions, and vice versa. By hunching over and hanging your head, you are silently advertising your lack of self-worth (even if you don't actually feel that way). Look at yourself right now; if someone were to see you, what message would they be receiving about your state of mind?

Owning the fact that you are a good, worthy person will help you stand with pride. To help the process along, consider how you would feel if someone were to give you a medal for just being you. That's the way you want to present yourself in order to reduce your shyness and increase your ability to interact with other people.

I don't think you can be proud of yourself and shy at the same time. Perhaps in some very unusual situations, like getting praised for something you didn't do, but most of the time if you are feeling good about yourself, it is expressed in your body language and your facial expressions. A big smile, even if you've just gotten a parking ticket, can let those around you know that you can handle life's little upsets, and that in turn will increase their confidence in you and your likeability.

It reminds me of a line from *The Hunger Games: Catching Fire*, when the character Effie says, "Shoulders back, head held high, smiles on..." Even if you are fighting for your life, good posture can let everyone know that you are going to win. And even if the odds are not in your favor, you can weather the storm and prevail. Knowing this in your own heart and head will push your shyness away and allow your best self to stand up.

Today, no matter what else is going on, focus on practicing good, even impeccable, posture. At the end of the day take a moment to evaluate how you feel. I can virtually guarantee that you will see an increase in positive emotions and a decrease in your shyness. Remember that if it worked today, it will also work tomorrow.

68.

The Power of Personality

Everyone has at least one unique or defining personality trait. As a shy person, you may feel that you don't have much to offer in the personality department, or you may feel that people will never get to know the real you, your core personality, due to the handicap of your shyness. Fortunately, there are ways you can enhance your personality and allow it to shine through, even if you're shy.

We tend to become like the people we spend the most time with, so if you know someone whose personality you admire, try spending time with him or her. This way, the desired personality trait or traits will rub off on you. Another way to enhance your personality is to become active on social media. Although this is not a substitute for real-life interactions, this is a safe way to see how others showcase their unique personalities and will inspire you to do the same.

Think of some personalities that you admire and consider how you could learn from them. Is there a well-known person, a politician or celebrity, whose personality you find particularly compelling or interesting? Read up on that person to learn what made/makes him or her tick. Watching a movie with your favorite actor or taking an acting class yourself can also help you develop the personality traits you admire. Did you know that many actors are actually very shy people naturally? Ironically, they found expression for their personalities in a most visible way.

If you feel shy around people with strong or difficult personalities, you're not alone. List some of their traits and then think of what you might do to emotionally regulate yourself around such people. Tell yourself that you do not have to let people with strong personalities affect your mood. *You* are in control of how much energy you give to them. If you find yourself exhausted around someone with a strong personality, your shyness may get in the way of setting healthy boundaries. Plan ahead, and prepare yourself to set necessary boundaries when you know you will be meeting up with this person, and then set limits in conversations so that you are not left feeling emotionally drained.

69.

Primp

When you feel good about how you present yourself—your overall look, how you smell and how you're dressed—it's extremely empowering. Being well-groomed and well-put-together can help you battle your shyness in a big way. You'd be surprised at how a couple of compliments (or even admiring looks) can change the way you feel about yourself and embolden you to try some new things—perhaps even reach out to some new people.

There is something to that ZZ Top song, "Every Girl Is Crazy About a Sharp Dressed Man," and it applies to both genders. We are all visual creatures, and when you understand that 55 percent of communication is visual, it can help you see that your physical appearance, though admittedly superficial, also makes a difference in how you relate to others and how they perceive you.

Personally, I have taken casual to a new level—a low one. I am in my sweats in the winter and shorts in the summer. Even if I'm going out, jeans and a sweater are about all you can expect from me. The only time I put on a shirt with a collar is when I'm being paid, but understand that a lot of thought and energy go into how I present myself to an audience, and dressing the part is not only expected, it enhances the speech. The "professional look" can go a long way to making you feel that you know what you are doing, and that is a true confidence builder. It's hard to be shy when you look like a million bucks.

Sometimes, when we are not feeling great about ourselves, we can lie around in our pajamas and maybe not even bathe for a day or two. This can be a sign that some depression may be emerging and you are probably not planning on interacting with other people (or you'd get dressed appropriately). If you need a day off, that's okay, but if you are letting your shyness keep you looking socially unacceptable, you need to change this habit and jump in the shower. Now. Even if it's the middle of your day, a shower can change your perspective and help you get going. We all feel better when we are clean, and though it seems like a small step, it may be just the trick you need to get back on a positive path.

If you don't have clothes that make you feel like an Oscar winner, perhaps a trip to the store is in order. Having a personal shopper put together an outfit or even an entire wardrobe for you can make a big difference in your willingness to go out into the world. Many stores offer this service for free, so take advantage of it. Once you have your clothing in order, get up, shower, and put on that power suit. You will feel empowered. Allow that feeling to propel you to the next level. When you look like you know what you are doing, no one will even think you are shy.

70.

Protect the Child Within

Protecting the child within is paramount to helping you overcome your shyness because that's probably where it all started. It's hard for most people to know, but shyness often starts as a result of trauma; then it slowly creeps up on you. Remember your first day of school? Was it fun or terrifying? If the latter, you most likely kept to yourself in your early years to avoid the pain. It's understandable, and if your parents and teachers didn't help you out of your shell, you could still be wearing it. If this is true for you, the following exercise is for you. The benefits of neutralizing childhood issues are tremendous. Not only will it help you be more outgoing, but it will raise your self-esteem and inspire you to be more creative.

We have all heard about, and perhaps made jokes about, our inner child. Although the concept has evolved over the years, the idea that we are every age we have ever been, still holds water. If you can remember childhood pain, it will have an effect on how you deal with life as an adult. Taking a look at your inner child and having a positive conversation with him or her is another way of taking this practice deeper and making it more effective.

You may think that talking to yourself and listening to what comes from the heart of your inner child sounds a bit crazy, but it works. The process is not without sadness, but you can turn that sadness into joy when you start to see the good things that happened to you when you were young, as well. But you need to get through the some of the painful parts first.

If you have few memories from your childhood, this can be a sign that you are blocking some trauma. Not everyone who has difficulty remembering had a terrible childhood, but about one-third of us go through some type of emotional trauma when we are children. It can be as benign as a trip to the doctor's office for your first shot, or as malevolent as a physically abusive parent or sibling.

If you were victimized as a child, first know it wasn't your fault. Now you are an adult, it's necessary that the grown-up you take charge of this childhood pain and loss. If you need to feel and mourn your pain, then by all means do that. I recommend that you get some help with this from a licensed therapist, because processing this kind of pain can be overwhelming. Whether you go it alone or do it with the help of a therapist, though, the point is to get in touch with what hurt you so you can confront and, ultimately, overcome it. Once you have identified, the trauma in broad terms—for example, "My mother was mean to me"—you can then focus your energy on healing this shame. This will go a long way toward helping you to let go of being shy. You will start to understand that your shyness was a way of protecting yourself from that pain, and preventing it from ever happening to you again.

Seeing the truth from here on out is much easier. You are now in control of your life and the people who get to be in it. Your shyness was once a means of protection; now, it is replaced by an ability to set boundaries, such that you feel safe in the world. There is no longer a need for you to hide behind your shyness.

71.

PTSD

The wound is the place where the Light enters you.

—Rumi

Posttraumatic stress disorder (PTSD) consists of a set of symptoms related to experiencing or witnessing a life-threatening event. The symptoms of PTSD vary from person to person, and can include social avoidance and withdrawal. People with PTSD can appear to be quite shy and withdrawn due to their behaviors. If you witnessed or experienced some type of trauma in your childhood or adulthood and have never fully dealt with it, even if you don't have full-blown PTSD, you may feel controlled by your shyness, depending on which situations trigger responses in you.

Many people who suffer from PTSD manage to turn their bad experiences around. Some of them develop positive attitudes, make the necessary changes to move on with their lives, and are successful in overcoming their fears and shyness. When my clients are receptive to therapy and make a consistent effort to work toward their goals, they almost always make progress. I have seen clients treat their traumatic experiences as wake-up calls; somehow they are able to take advantage of the new opportunities and resources provided to them after their trauma.

For example, one client who had came from a close-knit family was abandoned by them after they learned of the traumatic event, which concerned something that was taboo in their culture. My client found herself standing alone. She had never done anything without her family when growing up, which led to her being extremely shy. After being rejected by her family, however, my client learned, out of necessity, how to socialize with others, something that was new and quite frightening to her. She told me that learning to make friends helped her with her shyness. She also got to know herself by spending some time alone without her family. She found herself becoming more social and taking on new challenges, such as returning to school and learning how to sew in her spare time. Avoidance is a common mechanism for processing trauma. This client was lucky enough to be able to re-enter society after a few months. The trials and tribulations she went through only strengthened her ability to beat her shyness.

Hopefully you've never experienced any trauma and never have to in the future. However, if a past trauma is contributing to your shyness and causing you to avoid interacting with others, think of ways to work through it. You can learn coping skills to help you relax, such as meditating or listening to music. Ask trusted friends or family members to join you in practicing your relaxation skills. Take walks or join a yoga class with someone.

Coping skills can help you manage your stressors and reinvent yourself. For tougher cases, therapeutic interventions can involve a combination of exposure, such as learning about how a traumatic event has affected you, and working one-on-one with a therapist in order to learn more positive ways of thinking about and responding to the event and triggers. This is also known as *cognitive restructuring*.

You don't have to let your past dictate your future. Let the light in.

72.

Public Speaking

Feeling embarrassment, even outright terror, during public speaking is normal. Such feelings can also be accompanied by unwanted physiological changes: blushing, shaking, sweating, and feeling faint or dizzy. None of these is conducive to making a good speech! A friend of mine was extremely shy and had great difficulty speaking in front of others, so he signed up for a public speaking course to help him. To his embarrassment, he completely failed the course, because when he had to give his speech, he stumbled over his words and even forgot them in places. My friend had to contend with all the physiological symptoms, too—the sweaty palms, the upset stomach, the whole nine yards. This shows just how difficult his shyness made the course for him. These physiological symptoms are also common in people who are shy in social situations. The situation only becomes compounded when the shy person has to speak in front of a group. The good news is that even if you're painfully shy, you can learn to speak in public comfortably.

A great way to do this is through systematic desensitization, or graduated exposure therapy, in which the person is gradually exposed to the fear stimulus as he or she learns coping and relaxation skills, until the physiological response diminishes and eventually extinguishes. Part of this may involve imagining positive outcomes to exposure to the scary thing—in this case, public speaking—so that positive emotions are associated with the stimulus rather than negative, imagined responses and outcomes. As you can imagine, this has wide applicability for all kinds of fears, anxieties, and phobias. Flooding is another technique that has been proven to help people with phobias, although, as the name implies, it is a dramatic and much less comfortable process for the patient than graduated exposure. Flooding relies on the fact that the adrenaline and fear response only lasts so long. The idea is to get the patient past that point as he or she is exposed to the stimulus.

73.

Put Yourself Out There

There are some amazing people in this world who, against all odds, have managed to overcome seemingly impossible setbacks. No one would fault any of these individuals if they had chosen differently and decided not to put themselves out there in the world, yet they chose a different path in order to make a difference. Think about Stephen Hawking, perhaps the most brilliant man on the planet at the moment. Do you know what he does? A lot more than write books that most mere mortals can't fully comprehend. He tours! Yes, he gets on planes with his breathing apparatus, his wheelchair, and everything else he needs to stay alive and goes to cities all over the world. Remember that he cannot speak and uses a computer to relate his thoughts. Talk about putting yourself out there! Here is a man who could have easily kicked back and rested on his laurels—his multiple higher degrees, his many published books, and so on— but instead he puts himself through a great deal of effort and discomfort to bring his message to others.

Mr. Hawking can function as a shining example to those of us who deal with shyness. He doesn't let his disability stop him; he kicks it to the curb and creates his own destiny. And honestly, if he can do it, so can you.

Finding people who inspire you is pretty easy if you just look around, but sometimes seeing others succeed just reminds you of how stalled your own life is right now. Know that you have the power to change that. Yes, it's scary, but you are the only one who can make things different. No magical person is going to walk up to your door and tell you that your life is going to be much more joyful from here on out. A lot in life can be delivered or done for you, but if you want good feelings, you have to create them and chase them. And no, you don't need to be a world-famous physicist.

Whenever I tell a shy person to put himself out there, even just a little, I can see the discomfort and fear. It's usually mostly about rejection and looking bad in front of others. The key is to help him realize that by not stretching himself to be more involved with life, he is actually making a choice to live one of sadness. No, it won't kill him, but that's not the way anyone wants to live. You can get by if you give in to your shyness, but we all deserve a little joy, and you are no different.

I believe that Dr. Hawking really loves doing what he does. The discomfort and the inconvenience are not powerful enough to keep him from sharing his reality and inspiring millions around the globe. Just watching him give a speech or presentation will help you see that you, too, can accomplish what once was thought to be impossible. Seriously, watch a video of him: not only will you be impressed, but see if you don't gain some insights into your own life, as well.

You have more inside you than you ever thought possible. All you need is to put yourself out there and see where the journey takes you.

74.

Reasons We Let Shyness Stop Us

When it comes to achieving your dreams, what's stopping you? Because you picked up this book, I bet shyness has a lot to do with it. There are millions of reasons shy people don't take their shot at happiness. Here are a few of the big ones:

- **You feel you don't deserve it.** If you have doubts about your worthiness when it comes to life and interpersonal relationships, you need to take a long look into your internal mirror. What negative messages are you sending to yourself? Why do you believe that you are not good enough? Asking yourself these questions will help you develop positive alternative thoughts. Remember that you deserve happiness.
- **You question your ability.** You may be able to ask for what you want, and you may feel you deserve it, but you still wonder if you're up to the task. Maybe you think you don't have the talent or the leadership ability to get the job done. If you feel this way, you may need to just dive in and expect to make a few mistakes along the

way. As they say, an expert is someone who had made every mistake there is in his or her field.

- **You don't have the time to take on anything else.** Everyone I know who has successfully started their own business began working on it in their spare time. Evenings and weekends are no longer spent in front of the television (except maybe during football season). You can spend your extra time building your dream (or dating him or her). Anything you want to achieve is worth the extra work and investment of time.

- **You tell yourself that there's always someone who is better than you.** There will always be people who are better looking, who have more money, who boast higher degrees from better schools, and who have more scintillating personalities. But they aren't the same as you. You bring your *own* talent, personal vision, and values to any situation. Comparison is the thief of joy. Trust that what's inside you is as good as it gets.

- **You're trying to keep a low profile.** You may think that it's better not to stand out, because you're afraid you might get hurt. Yes, successful people can become targets for others who are angry, misguided, or jealous. But believing that harm will come your way if you're successful is a myth that was started by people who were too scared to reach for their dreams.

Does any of this sound familiar? You have the talent, the energy, and the gifts to fulfill your dreams. Don't let yourself or anyone else talk you out of going for it and fulfilling your heart's desire.

75.

Rebuilding Confidence

Sometimes a difficult experience or event can shatter your confidence. So can discouraging words from loved ones: they mean well, but maybe they said something that deflated you and made you wonder why you even try. Any number of things can cause us to doubt our abilities and ourselves. If you feel that your confidence has been shaken or even destroyed altogether, it's time to rebuild.

The recession shook the confidence of the entire world not too long ago. We are finding our way back slowly, even as many are still struggling to make ends meet and take care of their loved ones. When people fall on hard times, it's imperative that they don't go it alone. Community is always important, but never more so than when the chips are down. Likewise, the positive support from the important people in our lives will help us return to a place of internal security and confidence. When we don't have a good emotional support system in place, it makes it much harder to find our balance again. The power of having people who believe in you close by when you are going through a lapse in confidence is irreplaceable. This is really what having friends and family is all about. Life is so much better when we feel we have a team behind us—even if that "team" only consists of one other person.

It's wonderful and necessary to have good people in our lives who have our backs, but it's still incumbent upon us to call upon and use our inner strength. Amelia Earhart once said that the "most difficult thing is the decision to act; the rest is merely tenacity. The fears are paper tigers. You can do anything you decide to do. You can act to change and control your life; and the procedure, the process, is its own reward." But if you don't choose to be proactive, you become a victim of whatever circumstance is working you over right now. You have the power within you to make your life better.

Sometimes reaching down and finding your inner strength entails making sacrifices. It can also mean that your lifestyle changes, and that is hard for anyone, but it is better than letting the people and circumstances nip at your heels for the rest of your life. If you don't harness your inner strength, along with the support of those who believe in you, it will be impossible for you to dig your way out of this confidence hole. And make no mistake: it is work to rebuild confidence once it's been shaken or even toppled.

Confidence is of course an important part of feeling good about yourself, but it also helps others feel good about you. When you're confident and self-reliant, you let the people who are supporting you know that they have a teammate; you are in this up to your eyeballs and will not let them—or, more importantly, yourself—down. When everyone works together it makes the entire process easier and more effective.

Rome wasn't rebuilt in a day, but the joint effort will be worth it. And perhaps someday you can function as someone else's support system when his or her own confidence has taken a hit. That's a way to take something bad and make it work for good, in your life and the lives of others.

76.

Rejection Is Protection

I have been rejected more times than a nerd at the prom. Casting directors and record companies in my youth, publishers and editors after that: I have enough rejection letters to paper the halls of Congress. And let's not even talk about being the strikeout king of college dating. I guess you could say that I should be used to it at this point. Funny thing is that even with success, positive feedback, and actually growing a thicker skin, I am still sensitive to rejection. Most people are, and here's why: it almost always hurts a little. And for someone who is shy, just the thought of rejection is enough to keep you from even leaving the house.

When someone doesn't like you or your work and tells you straight-up, it stings. Even when it's soft-pedaled, there is still the visceral response. Your insides cringe a tiny bit and your shyness gets reinforced. Reacting this way doesn't mean you are a wimp, and it's no reflection on what you have to offer. It is simply your reaction to one person's subjective opinion and his or her tact (or lack thereof) in how he or she tells you.

It has been said that "rejection is protection," which means that you are probably better off not having this person in your life. Do you really want someone who doesn't want you? Most people pursue those who reject them because it's a challenge or because they just can't take no for an answer. I think it's a waste of time. And anyway, why would you even consider hanging out or working with someone who isn't 100-percent on your team? Don't put yourself on sale!

Another old saying that has proven true for millions is that "when one door closes, another opens." Yes, there are usually many more opportunities out there, but you have to look for them. If one rejection sends you into a tailspin or causes you to take to your bed for days, there may be something deeper going on. Don't get me wrong. I know how bad it hurts, especially if you have been in a long-term relationship, friendship, or job. But if you don't want to stay stuck in the muck, mire, and pain, you have no choice but to keep moving forward. Even if you're still reeling from a recent rejection, part of your head and heart must remain open to what is around the corner. Chances are it will be much better than what you just left behind. Sometimes these things happen so you have an opportunity to create the life you really want. Focusing on "what's next" will keep your shyness from stopping you.

Being left at the altar or let go from a job you love can feel like the end of the world—but it's not. Yes, your feelings count and they must be honored. Thinking, talking, writing, and crying are all things that can help ease the pain. It's wise to take your time before looking for the net best thing, but don't let too much grass grow under your feet. I suggest that after a brief period, you get on with your life. Embrace your newfound freedom and see where it takes you!

77.

SAD, Shyness, and Substance Abuse

As of this writing, there is still quite a bit of controversy regarding the legalization of marijuana. On the one hand, marijuana is known to have a plethora of medical benefits, everything from reducing anxiety in social settings to alleviating neuropathic pain, nausea, and symptoms of multiple sclerosis. On the other hand, there is always the specter of addiction to contend with. It is common for extremely shy people or those with social anxiety disorder (SAD) to engage in some type of substance use to alleviate their symptoms.

Many of my clients who are shy and uncomfortable in social settings have admitted to using marijuana to help with this problem. They say that marijuana helps them calm down, relax, and forget about past trauma. Smoking and drinking are social lubricants, and you may gain a greater sense of acceptance among your peers for joining them in substance use. But keep in mind that your inability to use these social lubricants at work can make socializing there more difficult. As well, marijuana has long-term effects and risks, just like any controlled substance. There exists a very high correlation (according to some estimates, as high as 40 percent) between marijuana use and SAD—a level at which it can have negative effects and can lead to more serious problems with substance abuse. Marijuana impairs cognition just as alcohol does. Also, it can sometimes have the opposite effect of what was intended, causing the user to stay home more often and turn down opportunities to socialize.

If your use of any substance has caused you to become more homebound, not less, reach out to a local 12-step group. Healthy support groups are one way you can engage in social activities and obtain social support during your journey to quitting. If attending events alone is too difficult for you, develop a support system of friends and family members who are willing to go with you. This way, you won't find yourself home alone too often or needing to smoke or drink alcohol to deal with your shyness.

78.

Seize Opportunities

There is an old saying that opportunity only knocks once. I don't believe it. I don't think it knocks at all. I believe that opportunity is lurking outside your door, in disguise, and you have to find it and actually drag it kicking and screaming into your house. For a shy person, this could seem next to impossible, but it isn't.

This is a case where your shyness could be of some benefit because it makes you pickier. You just don't want any opportunity; you want the one that is right for you and that fits your personality. Say you are looking for a new job. If you aren't the most outgoing person in the world, being in sales may not be your best bet, so if that opportunity comes your way, you should consider passing it up. But if an opportunity arises for you to work in a quiet, anxiety-free environment with a few supportive people, that may be the one to grab. The same thing goes for relationships. If you meet someone who is fun and attractive but really likes to go out and be the life of the party, that may not be the best person for you to date. Better you should take your time and look for a person who is more interested in the same things you are and with whom you have a connection. For a shy person, it can be hard to be around someone who likes to whoop it up and dance on the table.

Exercise

The fear factor here can be high, so try it slowly and gently at first. If you meet someone you want to know better, start with an e-mail to see if there is some mutual interest. If all goes well, have a brief conversation on the phone. If *that* goes well, ask to meet for coffee; leave the long dinner dates for later, if and when you're more comfortable. If it's a job opportunity, ask for an informational interview where you just talk about the company and yourself casually, just to see if there is a fit. Remember to be gentle with yourself and with the other people, as well—they may be shy, too! A good rule of thumb is to treat everyone the way you would like to be treated.

Wonderful things pass our way every day. Unfortunately, even though these things may be desirable, shy people find it difficult to summon up the energy to go after them. Reach into your heart and find the strength to grab onto the opportunities outside your door. Now go explore the very next opportunity that comes your way. Even if it's not right, the practice will help you be better for the next one.

79.

Self-Care Makes You Confident

Do you go out of your way to avoid drawing attention to yourself? Do you eschew makeup, bright colors, fashionable clothes, or bold, notice-me accessories? Is your favorite color gray? Grooming and adorning yourself can affect your mood in a positive way, though, so don't be too shy or afraid to experiment. Caring for yourself by spending a few extra minutes in the morning and putting on a fabulous watch, a new tie, or some pretty jewelry will not only make a big difference to your mood, but it can help improve your self-confidence, as well. If you are afraid of drawing attention to yourself because you are shy, you are not alone. Just remember to take baby steps and be yourself; you don't want to change your entire look overnight, as that would feel strange for anyone.

Most of us already have the things we need to enhance our appearance hiding at the back of our closets. Make an effort to rotate your clothes or separate them by seasons. When you get ready in the morning, add an accessory or two, such as a nice watch, a pocket square, some nice earrings, or a pretty scarf. Accessories are an easy way to update a stale wardrobe; they can also bring a more youthful vibe if the contents of your closet seem stuck in another decade. They are also an easy and inexpensive way to adopt the newest fashion trends without making over your entire look. Additionally, if you plan your outfits ahead of time and have your accessories organized, it can reduce the anxiety you feel when you are in a hurry to get dressed in the morning.

Ask yourself what bold new things you can do in your self-care treatment plan: would you like to color or straighten your hair? Grow some trendy sideburns? Have more youthful-looking skin? Lose weight? Invest in some new, fun products to take care of your skin and hair. Join a gym. Start walking every day. List some self-care tips you can follow to increase your self-esteem, such as getting a haircut or manicure, buying a new coat, or getting a massage. It's just a fact that when we look good, we feel good about ourselves. The most valuable thing you can do in your life is invest in yourself. And this isn't just about appearance. You can invest in yourself through education, by reading self-help books (like this one), or by taking a class and learning a new skill.

Don't be surprised if, after making some changes, you start getting compliments. Although it may feel awkward and even embarrassing—after all, you've now done the very thing you didn't want to do: draw attention to yourself— tell yourself that it is okay to receive positive attention, and remind yourself that it is your opinion of yourself that matters the most. Remember, shy people need self-care, too.

80.

Self-Fulfilling Prophecies

At some point in out lives, we have all rejected someone or been rejected ourselves. Failing to meet someone's expectations can be so painful that we end up living in fear. Unfortunately, these fears often become self-fulfilling prophecies in that we end up causing the very thing that we are trying to avoid. Self-fulfilling prophecies are unhealthy ways of thinking that involve treating an event as a foregone conclusion, directly or indirectly, before it occurs. When self-fulfilling prophecies are negative, they can contribute to the many attributes of shyness, such as low self-esteem, social phobia, and social anxiety.

Although self-fulfilling prophecies feel powerful, the actual correlation between expectation and outcome is only about 25 percent. Basically this means that magical thinking doesn't necessarily make it so. So no matter that your expectations are, remember that you are in charge of approximately 75 percent of your happiness.

Exercise

Try some mindfulness exercises to develop non-judgmental focus on yourself, rather than expectations, by meditating in your spare time. Close your eyes and think of a peaceful scene in which you feel relaxed. Some statements that can be useful if you find yourself engaging in self-fulfilling prophecies include "Maybe I'm jumping to conclusions," "Let's wait and see what happens," and "Why don't I give it a chance before I judge?"

Mind-reading is another unhealthy way of thinking, in which we believe we know what someone else is thinking just by analyzing his or her tone of voice, body language, and behavior. There are many ways to reduce your tendency to mind-read, such as thought-stopping or thought-blocking techniques. For instance, you might think that someone is upset with you because they don't seem as engaged in conversation as usual. It may be inappropriate to confront her at the moment, though, and you might feel uncomfortable asking her directly. If you can't confirm your feeling, just tell yourself some positive things to alleviate your anxiety. Say things like "She is always so nice to me" or "We've always gotten along well; maybe she's having a bad day."

As we get older, we tend to look to past experiences in order to make present ones better. It is valid to use experience to avoid bad mistakes. However, if you are judging a book by its cover, you should first weigh the pros and cons. If the cons exceed the pros, then you may have a valid reason. Just remember: getting over your shyness can start with eliminating negative, self-fulfilling prophecies. It is never too late to break the cycle that is preventing you from exploring new things with an open mind.

81.

Self-Handicapping

Self-handicapping is a cognitive strategy of avoidance. For example, if you don't feel you're up to the hard work of putting yourself through school, you may tell yourself that you would never be able to hold down a job and study at the same time. There are several reasons someone might self-handicap, including fear of rejection, a desire to avoid disappointment, and previous bad experiences or traumas. Self-handicapping can eventually become a shield for a shy person, blocking out both the bad and the good.

Someone I worked with once told me that she isolated herself because she was afraid of rejection. Her shyness and anxiety had prevented her from working for several years, but eventually she was forced to find a job and move into her own apartment. With time, she gained the strength and confidence to enter the job market, and she got a couple of interviews. During her first interview, however, she was too nervous to speak, and found her mind going blank even when she was asked questions she knew the answers to. She became so overwhelmed that she told the interviewer that she couldn't continue and ended the interview on the spot. At her second interview, she was hired with the condition than she would be on probation for her first 30 to 60 days. My client was so overwhelmed by the thought of future rejection that she effectively handicapped herself—declared herself unable—and declined the offer. Declining the job offer with no proof of the outcome was a form of self-handicapping that effectively prevented her from succeeding.

Shy people often rationalize avoiding a situation by saying they would rather not risk getting hurt. It is normal to do this, but remember that if you are unwilling to take the chance that your feelings will be hurt, you will only become more sensitive to *being* hurt. Studies have found that men are more likely than women to become withdrawn and avoidant when they feel rejected, especially when the rejection comes from a female they don't know. That said, everyone hates rejection. If you have handicapped yourself due to rejection, remind yourself to think positively and imagine ways in which you can use rejection to build resilience and gain strength for what you are seeking in life.

Exercise

Before jumping out of bed in the morning, think out your day. Slowly play out in your head what you will do, hour-by-hour. While you are relaxed, think of a situation in which you used self-handicapping to avoid a situation. Now think of ways in which you could have chosen to do something different instead. Now imagine enjoying the positive outcome.

81.

Self-Medication and Shyness

Because of the emotional pain that often comes along with being shy, many shy people choose to self-medicate that pain with alcohol or drugs. The majority of these substances are depressants; others actually increase arousal and anxiety. Drinking or smoking or pill-popping away your shyness is a dead end. Far too many people sit alone in their homes or rooms and just drink the night away because they are too scared to reach out to another human being. Drugs and alcohol can give you a false sense of bravery, but you won't be sober enough to do anything about it.

In addition, you can become addicted, which brings another very large set of problems along with it. Nothing like taking a lot of bad and adding a whole heaping portion of worse! Alcoholics and addicts live shorter lives and have less fulfilling relationships (if they have any at all), and many just hide from reality until they a) sober up, or b) pass away. Is this the life you want for yourself? Addiction to anything makes you selfish, and when you live that way, it pushes other people away. If you are a shy person who gets a lift from drinking or taking drugs, ask some friends if your personality changes when you are under the influence. You may not realize that you are behaving badly when you are high or drunk, and knowing that will help you stop the self-destruction.

The illusion that you are better, stronger, prettier, and so on when you are intoxicated may give you some false bravado and allow you to socialize in ways you can't when you are not self-medicating. The problem is that you will be your old self again very shortly and probably not feeling great about what you did the night before. Understanding that the effects are very temporary and will actually set you back emotionally may help you reconsider using substances to help you overcome your shyness.

A shy person with a substance abuse problem is setting himself up for more issues. Getting help can also be difficult as the shyness may keep you from seeking out support. If that is the case, individual counseling may be your best resource. It is interesting to note that 75 percent of people who get sober don't do it through traditional rehab or AA: they see an individual counselor. Make sure you find someone with experience in the field. An evaluation by a psychiatrist is also helpful. There may be a medication that can help with your shyness, but rest assured that drugs and alcohol are not it.

> The telephone number for The National Drug and Alcohol Treatment Referral Routing Service is 800-662-HELP. You can find The Substance Abuse Treatment Facility Locator online at *www.findtreatment.samhsa.gov.*

The bottom line is that alcoholism or drug addiction directly affect your ability to have good relationships, and no good relationship can survive them. If you want to keep what you have or expand your horizons, it's worth giving up the habit for good.

83.

Shyness and Relationships

If you are shy and you let it keep you from connecting with others, you're probably pretty lonely. The scary part of being lonely is it can actually shorten your life. The psychological stress that comes from that kind of pain weakens your immune system and unfortunately makes you physically vulnerable to opportunistic diseases. In addition, the loneliness can cause you to make unwise decisions and perhaps involve yourself with people who are not looking out for your best interests and who could even be dangerous. Not only have I seen it happen, it's happened to me.

When we are feeling that there is no one out there for us, and we have to go through this wonderful but challenging world all by ourselves, it can cause us to want to pull the covers up over our heads and stay in bed all day. Millions of people do just that. Some call it depression, others, addiction;

a few are just waiting to die, and that is no way to go through life. Life is meant to be lived—and not all by yourself.

Shy or introverted people actually *thrive* on emotional and conversational depth. They just don't necessarily know it. Not having someone to talk to on an intimate level is quite devastating, perhaps even as painful as never being touched or held. The need to connect is human, and those who cannot bring themselves to reach out are making the choice to be emotionally malnourished.

Having fulfilling relationships is a very difficult thing for many "normal" people to do successfully, but if you are shy, it can feel next to impossible. The idea here is to understand that a third to one-half of all people are shy, introverted, or living in fear of being rejected or judged. There are many out there just like you. Maybe they are even waiting for someone just like you.

The two major symptoms of depression are feeling hopeless and helpless. If you are neither then you have the strength to reach out to a friend or counselor and ask for a little coaching. If that feels too embarrassing, the Internet is a great place for the shy to meet, but beware that people are often less than honest when they are on the Web. Always use discretion. Sometimes just reading the articles on dating sites such as Match.com can prove to be helpful, with tips and tactics about conversing with a new person.

The truth is that if you really wanted to be alone, you wouldn't be reading this book so stop telling yourself that "you're okay flying solo." Many people live their entire lives telling themselves lies when all they need to do is to take an honest look in their mental mirror to get in touch with their true feelings. You are not destined to live a life feeling lonely, but no one can get you out of that pit but you. You have to make the first move. Now put your loneliness on hold and make that call!

84.

Shyness and Not Being Nice

Shy people have a reputation for being quiet and retiring. People assume that a shy person will stand at the back of the room and not ask questions. Most see shyness as a harmless personality glitch that a few unfortunate people have to deal with, but there are many more shy people out there than anyone knows, and what they are dealing with is very painful and very real. One way many shy people get past their shyness it is by being unpleasant. For them, the best defense is a good offense, and offensive they are.

It's hard to make it in life if you're not nice to others. Yes, there are a few sadistic folks out there who get off on making people suffer, but for those of us who are generally emotionally fit, if you're treating people in a shabby manner, you aren't going to feel very good about yourself. If you have engaged in this type of behavior, it may be because you are overcompensating for your shyness unconsciously. Try taking a step back and see if you can put your finger on as to why you aren't being your nicest self. Is it fear that is causing you to be defensive or aggressive? Are you in a situation that is making you feel uncomfortable? Either of these can cause you to project a harsh personality as a means of protecting yourself. Most of the time, you probably don't know you're doing it, so the best way to find out what is actually going on is to ask people.

Being the nice guy (or lady) doesn't mean that you have to do what everyone else wants. Moreover, you don't have to buy people things or accept other people's bad behavior. Being nice simply means being your best self with a little kindness thrown in. Remember that old saying "It's not what you say, but how you say it"? That is the essence of niceness. You say and do things in a way that doesn't offend, upset, or anger anyone else. You choose not to be the cause of their unhappiness. Instead, you are encouraging, emotionally available, and willing to help if necessary. By presenting yourself in a nice way, you also magically defuse any negativity that might be coming at you.

When it comes to getting past shyness, the power of niceness is tremendous. That little bit of warmth can be felt by others; when it is returned to you (again, unconsciously) it makes your shyness disappear. This silent exchange of emotional currency is one of the bedrocks of overcoming shyness. Your mission is to remember all the nice things people have said about you and take them in. Let those compliments convince your brain that you are a very nice person indeed. To the extent that you believe that, others will want to engage with and relate to you. Although this is mostly an internal process, you also need to practice with people. Tomorrow, regardless of what you have planned, put your nice self in gear and smile at everyone you come into contact with. You also might want to say a few nice things to coworkers or family. Sow those seeds of kindness and watch what grows from them.

85.

Shyness and Suffering in Silence

Perhaps one of the most difficult things in life is getting some bad news and having no one to share it with. If you're suffering right now, you may feel that your shyness won't allow you to reach out to another person, even a family member, so that you can share the difficulty, sadness, or shock you may be feeling. We all have bombs dropped on us from time to time, and one of the best ways to cope with it is to talk to someone, but for a shy person this can feel next to impossible.

If you feel too embarrassed to share what has happened, your desire to keep up appearances may not be serving you here. If you hold it all in, you could make yourself physically ill. It is very important to share your experiences, even or especially the negative ones, so that you can (a) get an outside perspective, and (b) let out some of the pain. When you hold everything in, you won't function as well. Sometimes you may feel like a bowling pin: being set up just to get knocked down again. We all have periods in our life when that happens and we feel we just can't get a break. But sharing your experience, though you may feel uneasy about opening up, can make a big difference in how you cope. Bringing another human being into the picture, even if he or she has nothing to do with your situation, helps you by offloading some of the emotional burden.

These are the times when silence is not golden, but cheap brass. Holding on to what is bothering you will work against you in long run. We have made more than 100 suggestions in this book about how to overcome your shyness, but in this case you don't need to be rid of it to reach out to someone. Just understand that simply sharing what's going on in your life lessens the burden you're carrying. It also provides you with another perspective and new insights as to how to deal with your problem. Putting your shyness aside can be a challenge, but the insecurity that comes from making yourself vulnerable to someone is outweighed by the relief you will feel from letting it all out. If you truly have no one to talk with, seeing a professional is perfectly acceptable. In fact, it may be better for you because not knowing the person and having the confidentiality can make you feel safer sharing your feelings.

We are all faced with challenges in our lives, but to deal with them all by ourselves is tantamount to torture. Even though it is frightening to talk with another person, especially about something that is very personal, it is without a doubt one of the best things you can do to move your life forward again. So pick up the phone and call someone to talk about your troubles for a few minutes. The person you call will feel honored that you reached out and trusted him or her, and you will feel better letting go of what has been bothering you.

86.

Shyness and the Holidays

People who suffer from shyness often feel all alone in the world. That kind of loneliness is depressing anytime, but during the holidays, the sadness is heightened and brought into sharper focus as you compare yourself to all of those seemingly happy and joyous people around you. Even the commercials can be depressing, with attractive and terminally happy people partying it up and having a great time. Everyone seems to have having a great time but you. This is when it becomes necessary to take care of yourself by breaking out of your shell and reaching out to others.

A great way to do this is by volunteering in your community. There are so many people out there who have nothing—families that don't have enough money to put food on the table, let alone buy their children gifts and toys. Not only will you make a difference to people who need you, but you will meet others who are caring and perhaps in need of some company, as well. The positive feelings you get from helping others will diminish your shyness because you feel needed and wanted. The self-esteem you get from being a caring and empathic person can never be taken away. Many people who suffer from shyness work in the public sector to help those in need simply because of the warmth they receive in return from the people they help.

It's very important that you do not choose to isolate. Even just going to the mall or to a place of worship will help bring in a little more of the holiday spirit and reduce your shyness. If you find yourself invited to parties, by all means, go, and toast the festive season with some new friends. Whatever you do, though, don't go to a bar and try to drink away your feelings of sadness and isolation. It will only warm you temporarily, and then you'll wake up feeling exponentially worse each time you choose this path. Remember that alcohol is a depressant; if you're already feeling down, it's just going to amplify any negative feelings you may be having.

Expressing forgiveness and acceptance is a big part of what the holidays are all about. If some of your relatives have always acted out or made you feel badly, chances are that won't change. If you know what you're getting into, it will be easier to not let them push your buttons. If things get uncomfortable, take a time out and go to a movie or for a drive and adjust your response. People say and do hurtful things to one another for no reason at all. Aunt Martha may have had a little too much eggnog, and your cousins could be spending most of their time on their cell phones, but that isn't what this season is about. Learning to enjoy and even laugh at the people you are close to can be a challenge, but it is something you can accomplish with some practice. The real truth is that it is better to be with people with whom you can have some positive interactions than to allow yourself to wallow in your own self-pity by sitting all alone. It may not be perfect, but it sure beats being by yourself!

87.

Shyness as Safety Net

Most people who are shy have been hurt and have suffered social injuries, whether through rejection or humiliation in front of others. Shy people who have been rejected or hurt in the past are more likely to shut themselves off from others because they are afraid. The psyche has a built-in mechanism for avoiding pain. We use this mechanism to protect ourselves from injury. It is natural to want to avoid unpleasant events. This is why people who have experienced traumatic events tend to avoid talking about them. When we are reminded of an unpleasant event or experience, it can bring further pain by causing us to relive the experience. If you are shy, you may believe that if you stay away from others entirely, you can keep yourself from being hurt again. The idea of a safety net may sound appealing, but if you build a wall around your heart, you may end up hurting those closest to you by keeping them away.

Some people believe that you get back what you put out into the universe. Whether you call it karma, the law of attraction, or some other name, the basic premise is the same: you reap what you sew. If you do not allow others to draw close to you, you may start to feel a lack of support from them in return. One of my clients was afraid of getting involved in a romantic relationship. His defense mechanism—his "wall"—was to keep so busy with his job that even when he met someone interesting, he would have no time for that person. Instead of going out to dinner or a movie, he would brag that he had to work overtime or during the holidays. When he did have time off, he would visit his family and spend time with them. Eventually people started avoiding him even though, deep inside, he longed for a relationship.

I helped him recognize his defense mechanism for what it was and hear what he was telling himself: *As long as I am busy, I can avoid becoming emotionally involved and, hence, keep myself from getting hurt.* He thought that he was preventing further pain, but he was actually creating pain because he was constantly lonely. He finally admitted that his being alone was his own fault because he wanted to be safe. Once he recognized the real cause of his loneness, he could work on himself.

If you are shy and you fear getting hurt because of a past negative experience, try telling yourself that the past doesn't define you or your future. If you are shy because you were hurt in the past, ask yourself what you learned from that experience that could help you in a future relationship. If you can use the wisdom that you gained from your experience, you will not have to feel as though you wasted your time on something that you can never get back. As the saying goes, "Those who do not learn from history are destined to repeat it."

88.

Shyness in the Workplace

Shyness can be a real handicap in the workplace. Most days you may feel that you are more of an observer than a participant. However, lack of involvement and engagement can cause you to lose out on opportunities.

Perhaps you experienced an embarrassing situation at work, such as having an opinion or idea pushed to the side during a meeting, and you told yourself afterward that you would never speak up again. You should know that refusing to engage in a desirable behavior can be habit-forming and can contribute to your overall avoidance of social activities in general. Conversely, the more you engage in social activities at work, such as lunch meetings, seminars, and discussions, the more the pleasure system in your brain will reward you. It may sound counterintuitive, but it's true.

Perhaps you've heard the saying that closed mouths don't get fed. This is especially true in the workplace. If you feel that you deserve a promotion, why not come up with a presentation and ask your boss if the two of you can meet? Plan ahead by having organized your thoughts well before the meeting. Be prepared to answer questions, and draw attention to the skills and attributes that you bring to the job. Even if you are shy, you can push for a promotion by listing the ways in which you improve the company and help it flourish. If your boss can see the profit you are bringing to the table, she will probably be willing to hear you out.

When you are speaking with your boss, or even with your coworkers, don't be afraid to ask questions. If someone doesn't agree with your point of view, don't take it personally. When one door closes, another one opens. Remember, even if you didn't get the promotion you were looking for, you can look for other ways to improve that will put you in good stead for future promotions and raises. Your listening skills can take you a long way in this regard. Try to understand what your boss wants, and make her working style your own.

Exercise

At the end of each workday, identify five positive feelings that you felt during the day. Make a list of any opportunities at work that you'd like to take advantage of but have been too shy to pursue until now. Now list some of the ways you could seek support in accomplishing your goals. Sometimes we need the input of friends and family members in order to realize our opportunities and our worth.

Shyness does not have to control your life at work. You are in charge of your happiness both on and off the job.

89.

Shyness Reduction Techniques

When your shyness feels like it's having its way with you, there are a number of things you can do to decrease the tension and get back to life as you know it. Remember that you can feel panic even if the source of your shyness is not immediately present, because sometimes stress just floats out there for a little while, trying to get your attention. This is called *ambient anxiety*. You have more power over your fear and anxiety than you may think. The following exercises will help you feel better about yourself when you're feeling really stuck. The first one involves getting your shyness out on the table. If you are in a relationship, you can do this exercise with your partner. You also can do it with anyone in your life who is a good listener.

- Step 1: Look at and talk about the worst-case scenario. Get all your feelings and fears out so you know what you're dealing with. Be sure to discuss what you'd do in the worst-case scenario and how serious the consequences would be.
- Step 2: Talk about the best-case scenario and revel in all that it brings you. Take a moment

to really soak in all of the positive changes that could result.

- Step 3: Look at what's most likely to happen. While you can't be certain, it's reasonable to expect that most of these scenarios will fall somewhere in the middle of the worst- and best-case scenarios. Remember that the results are also largely dependent on your response to whatever happens.

Going through this process will decrease anxiety and help you embrace the positives in your life. Taking this tried-and-true action will yield positive results.

Be proactive about your shyness. Some people take supplements (a popular one is fish oil) or drink chamomile tea to help them relax. Daily exercise is also a great way to help you overcome the anxiety. So is meditation, if you would rather be less physically active. Avoid the news and watch a comedy instead. Events you see on TV or read in the papers may trigger your shyness about going out into the world. I'm not suggesting you live in a cave, but if you are having an anxiety-ridden day, it might be best to do something more pleasant than getting sucked into the latest bad news. Once you learn what brings on feelings that make you want to hide, it will help you avoid triggers in the future.

Revisit places that make you feel peaceful inside. Being by water or in nature is very calming for many people. Sometimes reading a book by the pool can be as good as reading one in the mountains. The trick is to find and then remember the places that make you feel most peaceful, and the next time you are feeling shy, go to a quiet spot and just imagine yourself back in your peaceful place. I know it sounds too simple, but it works very well.

Start your day on the right foot. When I wake up in the morning, the first thing I do is a brief meditation. Simply visualizing a peaceful day ahead and reminding myself that I am safe are helpful little tools that can make the difference between a nervous day and one of tranquility. I use this meditation technique throughout the day whenever necessary.

You don't have to allow shyness to have the upper hand. If these exercises don't give you enough relief, please see a medical professional. Many medications can be helpful, and even if you don't like the idea of taking pills, just talking with a doctor can be reassuring.

90.
Social Groups

If you are shy, there is still hope for you to reduce your fear of rejection by peers. The less you are exposed to your peers, and the more you lack interaction with social groups, the less likely it is that you'll be included and invited by others.

Participation in group activities, whether they involve business, sports, hobbies, or the arts, has positive long-term effects. Whether or not someone can take advantage of such activities probably stems from experiences during adolescence. If adolescents are not exposed often enough to social groups to learn the importance of friendships, they are likely to continue having difficulty maintaining social connections into their adulthood. It's not too late, though: we can make interacting with other people much less stressful just by participating in more social activities right now. More time spent with friends can benefit us because it helps us be impervious to social exclusion. If you spend more time with friends and stay engaged in social activities, you will be less sensitive and less stressed out when you do perceive a social threat or rejection.

If you opt out of events every time you feel shy, remind yourself that the more friends you have, the more friends you will make. Also, having and making friends will help you build resilience to rejection and reduce the stress you feel when you are rejected (it happens to everyone, after all). Simply put, the more friends you have, the more likely it is that you will have someone you can really count on. And remember that pain response that occurs when we are rejected? You should look for inexpensive ways to strengthen your neural response to rejection and increase your resilience. Do this by going on group hiking trips, joining a book club, or taking a class. If you take a class and you feel uncomfortable and shy, don't leave. Instead, stick around after class until you make a new friend, and exchange your contact information so that you can help each other with assignments.

If you are able to engage in social activities every week, it can be a great exercise to help you identify the emotions you feel when you are rejected. Keep a journal, and write down an entry every time you feel sensitive to a social rejection. Identify and describe your feelings. Then describe positive new ways in which you could have responded. Use this approach to be more open to rejection and even criticism. Have compassion for yourself and accept what applies and leave the rest. You cannot change a lonely, painful past, but you can make the future so much better when you are part of a community.

91.

Social Networking for the Shy

Using social networks is a great way to break out of your shyness. You can test the waters of various kinds of social situations by joining social network groups that interest you, such as ones for knitters, hikers, skiers, and gardeners. They even have ones expressly for shy people! If you attend a meet-up, you'll probably encounter someone else who is there for the first time, too. One of the best ways to blend into an event is to show up early and befriend other new people, because you are all in the same boat.

Befriending an existing member of a group is a great way to get introduced to other people in your new network of friends. Recent studies have shown that shy people tend to spend more time on online social networks, especially

Facebook (which, with more than 600 million members as of this writing, is one of the most popular online social networking sites). However, more socially confidant people tend to spend less time on social networking Websites because they are already busy enjoying the activities they love with friends.

After joining a network group and meeting up with potential new friends, you will start to learn about new activities, events, and other upcoming meet-ups. This is your opportunity to shine by venturing out of your comfort zone. Try saying yes to every event that you can realistically attend. If you follow through, you will increase your feeling of satisfaction with your life. Conversely, the more you decline invitations, the less likely it is you will be invited in the future. Although you may be truly busy, others might see your refusal as evidence of disinterest. To avoid this, try not to turn down every invitation you're offered.

One client that I worked with who was struggling with shyness found herself having more fears about socializing after graduating from college and relocating to a new town. She was afraid that everyone would know that she was a newcomer and that they would not be friendly because of this. She would get excited when she would learn of upcoming events in her town like dances or festivals. She would sign up enthusiastically and plan for the events weeks in advance, but when the time came to attend one of these events, she would automatically think of an excuse not to follow through with her plan.

Negative thoughts were getting in the way of her self-confidence, thoughts such as *I will be the only person attending this event alone* and *I am going to look like a loser if I go alone.* Therefore, she opted out of going to any events for several months. This changed one day when a mutual friend invited her to a pool party through Facebook. Although she didn't know if her friend would show up, she decided she would go to the party no matter what. When her friend backed out of going, my client was devastated and wanted to go home. However, she told herself how silly it would be to leave after the long drive. *Now that I'm here, I should at least check it out*, she thought.

She was so proud of herself as she walked past the entrance gates to the pool, that she immediately began to realize the benefits of attending an event alone. She was happy that she didn't need to tag along with friends and that she could leave whenever she wanted to without anyone becoming upset. To her surprise, furthermore, she ran into an old friend at the party and was introduced to two new friends. My client was able to see her social network group growing right in front of her eyes—all because she was willing to take that once chance.

No matter what group you find yourself a part of, always be your true self. Don't be afraid to be the first one to speak up in a new setting. Sometimes asking a simple question can spark a lively conversation. Additionally, try to eliminate negative thoughts—you know, the inner critic that tells you lies such as *I look like an idiot* and *Nobody here likes me*. These thoughts will increase your avoidant behavior and your fears. If you find yourself thinking negative thoughts, try repeating a few positive statements to yourself instead.

Remember that you have the power to eliminate shyness from your life, or at least make it a non-issue. Look for groups that can help you with your shyness and help you build your confidence. Who knows? Maybe one day you'll be organizing your own group, and you'll find a new, shy friend who needs help getting past her own shyness.

92.

Stand and Deliver

When you were in grade school, you may have dreaded being picked to read out loud. For example, when my client Jason was in middle school, his teacher would assign exercises in which each student had to read at least one paragraph to the class. Because he knew that his turn would come eventually, he would develop those fight-or-flight symptoms such as the sweaty palms and rapid heartbeat even before he had to do anything. He would try to prepare by reading the paragraph in his head to ensure that he wouldn't make any mistakes. When his turn came, he would always start off well, but somehow he always managed to stumble on a word before he'd finished the first sentence. This made him upset and embarrassed.

This sort of worry is commonly carried into adulthood. If you are shy and afraid of making mistakes during work presentations or social activities, you might want to bring your idea of perfection under control by reminding yourself that it's okay to stutter or mispronounce a word or several words. We sometimes become so fixated on the fear of making a mistake that it ultimately causes us, in a kind of self-fulfilling prophecy, to make one. The more we think about mistakes, the more likely we are to make them. In fact, sometimes we can feel relieved after making a mistake because we no longer have to worry about one—it's already happened!

Similarly, if you are uncomfortable with making eye contact, try not to think about the fact that you're making eye contact. Think of it as you would breathing: we usually don't think about the fact that we're breathing because it's something that our bodies do naturally and automatically.

Exercise

If you are shy about speaking in front of others, take a speech class at your local college or join your local chapter of the Toastmasters. Ask a close friend to help you practice speaking in front of others by doing speech exercises with you. One fun and helpful speech exercise is reading a play together: you each pick different characters and read your lines out to each other. Singing lessons are also helpful. They teach you to use vocal muscles that most people don't use very often, and this can give you a stronger tone and better control over your voice, thus increasing your confidence when you speak. If you commute to work, listen to audiobooks that ask you to repeat words out loud. Find a subject that interests you, such as a program to boost your vocabulary or an audiobook course on a language you'd like to learn.

The more you practice, the more comfortable you'll feel and the more familiar you will be with the way you sound. This is not practice for perfection, though, but for comfort, self-assurance, and the ability to stand and deliver.

93.

Socializing Tips for Introverts

I have a secret that I've kept from the public for almost my entire life: I am shy. Most people wouldn't guess it, but when I have to give a talk and meet new people, I usually don't get much sleep the night before. And if there is a meet-and-greet before the talk, I can become a nervous wreck, thinking about all those people I don't know and who don't know me, asking me questions and expecting me to be entertaining and informative. It can be a very scary proposition.

I'm the same way socially. If I'm invited to an event where I don't know many people—perhaps a party given by acquaintances of my other half—it can be a bit daunting to put on the public me rather than just be the guy who watches football on Sunday in his PJs. Trying to be that person can be wearying, but when required to, I can call the plays and help my partner by being a little more outgoing in social situations. Here are a few tricks that have worked for me and may help you, as well:

- **Try to keep a smile on your face.** This lets people know that you are open and receptive to being approached. Seeing someone smile helps the other person feel that you are safe to talk to.

Smiling also sends a signal to your own brain telling you that you are in a good place and should expect nice things to happen around you. It's interesting that we are the only species in the animal kingdom that bares its teeth as a sign of welcome and joy. Other species do it only when they are angry or scared (called *fear aggression*).

- **If you are talking to a small group of people who don't already know each other, become the master of ceremonies.** By that I mean be the one who makes sure that everyone gets properly introduced. If someone new comes along, you need to introduce him or her to the group, as well. This will help you get to know everyone and make conversation, though not necessarily about yourself. The other people in the group will appreciate your efforts. It makes you look like an outgoing person even if you are a little (or a lot) shy.

- **Use a person's name when you first meet.** When you are introduced to someone, call the other person by name as you shake hands. Say you are at an event and someone introduces you to a guy named Dave. Say, "Hi, Dave. Nice to meet you." It's a really simple action that produces some very powerful results. The person you are greeting will feel more welcome, you will remember the name after you've said it aloud, and you will feel more empowered and comfortable because you are in control of the situation and conversation. The next step is to ask Dave where he is from and what brought him to this event. The conversation will usually flow on its own from there.

Using these tips can make a potentially uncomfortable evening a pleasant one for those of us who are introverted. This stuff is easy and it works, so give it a try.

94.

Spirituality for the Shy

A religion is a system of beliefs, values, and practices that are adhered to by its members in order to create some type of spiritual relationship among themselves and with a higher power. Some people believe that religion brings balance and calmness into one's life. Joining a church, a temple, a mosque, or some other kind of spiritual organization is a great way to meet new people who may be shy, just like you. Participating in spiritual and religious activities can even help you govern the emotional regions of your brain, improving your memory-retrieval networks.

Places that provide opportunities for spiritual connections are great places to network and mingle. Most people who are connected to spiritual social groups feel less judged and are able to be themselves. These environments tend to be warm and welcoming, and they offer a great avenue to involvement in the community through volunteer work.

Many of these organizations also offer activities like choral singing and plays. Take advantage of this and participate in as many activities as your schedule allows. You will most likely meet other shy people and become more comfortable being yourself around them. This is a great thing. If you don't care for spiritual or religious affiliation, however, try thinking of other emotion-based rewards, such as volunteering at a hospital, participating in a fundraiser, or running a marathon for a great cause, such as cancer awareness.

Shy people are often afraid to show their emotions due to a fear of being judged or rejected. In many religious settings, however, emotions are regularly displayed. Joining such a community can help you tap into your emotional side in a positive way. You may be reluctant to put yourself in a situation where you might be called upon, which can happen when you are introducing yourself to a new group. Use positive self-talk, and tell yourself that there is nothing wrong with showing your emotions. Don't stay at the back of the crowd. Spiritual and religious communities are often welcoming rather than judgmental. Practice positive thinking, and reject any negative thoughts that pop into your head after you agree to take part in an activity.

Spirituality and religious connections have a big influence on our emotions, which is one area where shy people struggle. Becoming involved in the activities of these groups is one way of gaining confidence and conditioning yourself to being around others. If you can't find any activities that suit you, don't be afraid to propose your own activity or class. Religious and spiritual communities are always grateful to have new community members to enhance and expand their programs. If you have a skill you would like teach to others, start a class. The individual attention will not only increase your self-confidence and reduce your shyness, but it can also boost your ego. I call that a win-win!

95.

Take an Acting Class

For a shy person, just the thought of being on stage in front of an audience can be terribly frightening. That said, sometimes the only way through your fears is to face them. There are gentle ways to do that that will surprise you, keep your anxiety level under control, and greatly reduce your shyness. One of these ways is by taking an acting class

Whether it is a community college or city theater, the opportunities abound in almost every neighborhood for you to get involved in the dramatic arts. If you can imagine yourself on stage, if it is a dream you have kept hidden because of your shyness, this is an opportunity to move your life forward and stop being held back by your insecurity. There are several ways to do this. The least intimidating is to get involved with a local theater group as a support person, not an actor—yet. Those who put on shows need all kinds of help, everything from set design and make-up to public relations and ticket sales. If you aren't ready to audition for a part, just being around theater people will embolden you and provide you with the opportunity to make some new friends.

In addition to putting on plays and events, many theater groups also teach classes to help you *slowly* make friends with the stage. In a class I took many years ago, the first thing we did was wash the stage floor by hand. The teacher told us it was a way of getting in touch with our dreams and desires, and being that close to the stage just made it seem friendlier. Being on stage is an amazing experience; yes, you'll have butterflies in your stomach, but they are flying in formation. You need that excitement to give a good performance; what you will learn is how to channel that feeling in a way that empowers you and doesn't make you want to run away and hide. Once you have played a part on stage, in front of people, you will never be the same again, and the changes will all be positive ones.

For those who are still too uncomfortable to actually take a class or join a theater group, there are interactive and passive courses on the Internet. I don't think you will get the same results, or the same rush, but this is not a bad warm-up if it gets you in the door of your community theater or eventually has you take Acting 101 at the local community college.

This is also something that could prove very valuable to your children if they are dealing with shyness, too. Including them can also help you because you won't be totally focused on how you are doing or what other people are thinking; your attention will be where it should, on your kids. It's amazing how we can take cues from them, and because we don't want to look like wimps in front of our children, you may well take up the mantle and show the little ones how it's done.

Many groups offer single evening classes; if not, private coaches and schools are always putting on plays. Your mission is to walk into one of these places and ask when the next auditions are. This will be a huge healer for your shyness.

96.

Talk to Strangers

When I am asked to give a speech in a place I've never been, it's always an interesting and growth-producing experience. It almost always starts with me getting on an airplane and sitting next to a complete stranger. Sometimes there is good conversation, cards are exchanged, and the flight seems shorter. Other times, there is only a little chit-chat, and even more rarely, there's no conversation at all, just a silent struggle over who gets the armrest.

Once I've landed and made my way to the hotel, there is usually a "meet the speaker" dinner. The one person I will know (but most likely have never actually met) is the person who hired me. So here I am in a room full of strangers all wondering to themselves, "Who is this guy, and does he have anything worth saying?" The truth is that I feel the same way. Although many would describe me as an extrovert, I am actually a shy one. In a roomful of people I don't know and who expect me to be Dr. Personality, getting introduced, shaking hands, and making a little small talk can be a daunting task. After I give my speech the next morning, it's a whole different story. Then everyone knows me, and many will have questions and comments, which makes having a conversation so much easier. But before that happens, I have to find ways to talk with these folks, making them feel at ease and perhaps even interested in what I have to say.

In situations like this, it helps to have good interviewing skills. Asking the right questions is a great way to help people open up and feel good about meeting you. When you ask people about themselves, they are usually more than willing to share. Most people appreciate it when you show an interest in their lives. Another way to garner a good introduction and a little conversation with a stranger is to tell a story. Good storytelling is a powerful way to connect with others. The other person gets to respond to the story you've told or perhaps to offer his or her own story in response. Before you know it, someone has to leave, but you've had a good conversation and made a stranger into an acquaintance, and even a friend.

Talking with people you don't know isn't that hard. You don't have to be a great conversationalist. You just have to be willing to risk rejection, hold out your hand, and say, "Great to meet you. Have you ever noticed...?" and then tell the other person your best story or something you've recently discovered. The topic doesn't matter; it's your willingness to engage that will open the lines of communication. Of course, this also means giving the other person a chance to share his or her experiences, as well. Talking with people whom you don't know is a skill that most anyone can develop. You can practice with people you already know and then see how it goes at your next networking event, meeting, or party. Just remember that most people enjoy talking about the good parts of their lives, so keep it positive.

97.

Think Positive

How many times have you heard someone say, "Think positive"? I'm sure that someone has told you this at least once in your life, and they were probably saying it because you weren't thinking all that positively at the time. Sometimes we feel overwhelmed and stressed. If we are shy, we may perceive situations more negatively, and hearing someone say, "Think positively," may not be helpful at the time. In fact, it can feel more like an irritant and even a criticism.

There is no guarantee that positive thinking will change your situation. However, negative emotions do narrow your mind and focus your thoughts on bad things. Positive thinking opens up horizons and makes things look better. For instance, if you are shy and want to join a new social club in order to meet people, thinking negatively will cause you to give off nonverbal cues of low self-esteem. Unfortunately, low self-esteem is not a quality that will attract many new friends. Of course, awareness of your body language can help you reduce any negative non-verbal cues. But social groups also tend to want to hang around with people who think positively. Negative people will only bring down the positive energy of the group. So don't be a Debbie Downer. If you can't think of anything nice or positive to say, it's probably best to wait until you can.

A friend of mine who was extremely shy once tried his own brand of exposure therapy by joining a yacht club. He took part in their regatta events, and though he never had a team of his own, he would join new teammates all the time. He became part of a wonderful social group that had several other events during the year, such as fundraisers, dances, and breakfasts. Although he never won a race, that didn't stop him from getting up at 5 a.m. to prepare for them. Afterward he would have a beer and socialize with the team. Winning a regatta was not the ultimate reward. The reward was staying connected to his group, which brought him social rewards and created a safe environment for his shyness to transform into a more confident personality. He was able reduce his shyness by maintaining a positive attitude regardless of whether or not they lost the race.

Of course, things are rarely all bad or all good. The combination of negative and positive emotions is called ambivalence. Ambivalence can result in confusion and the inability to make a decision. Ambivalent attitudes have a correlation with unstable attitudes over time. It is important to think positively because negative emotions will prevent your brain from seeing any positive future. If you are shy and want to reduce your negative emotions, practice having positive emotions. That way, you can enhance your ability to develop skills that can be useful later in life.

98.

Travel Guidelines for the Shy

Many shy people who dream of traveling to a particular locale put that dream trip on hold because they can't find someone to travel with them. Those who are shy rarely want to travel alone. There's a big difference between traveling alone and traveling with a friend. Experiencing a special moment, walking to the Coliseum in Rome or taking the elevator up the Eiffel Tower in Paris, is quite different when you're with someone than when you're alone. This is because happiness is the only thing that grows when it is divided and shared. Creating special memories with those who are closest to us, those whom we love, is a wonderful bonding process. Traveling alone has its merits (have you read *Eat, Pray Love?*), but for a shy person, having a companion may be just the ticket.

If you have a place in mind that you would like to visit, think of a friend or two who might want to go along with you. Remember that people are busy, and that traveling requires some disposable funds. Don't let this stop you from fulfilling your travel dream, though. Look through local magazines in your town that may offer travel opportunities. You can also find out about meet-up groups that visit the places that interest you. Contact the group organizers and attend the next meeting. Getting to know a group before committing to traveling with them is definitely a good idea.

Don't discount traveling solo, either. In my experience, traveling alone is just as fun as traveling with large groups. During my first solo trip to Europe, I found myself lost and waiting at a train station in Amsterdam for nearly an hour. A lady who was standing next to me noticed that I looked confused and offered to help me get to the center of town. She said that she was familiar with the city and that I could tag along with her, since she had some time to kill. She was visiting Amsterdam for a conference, and I had a nine-hour layover.

I was delighted and accepted her invitation without hesitation. We took the train downtown and walked along the busy streets along the canals. The city was gorgeous, full of bikers and other pedestrians. I couldn't believe how lucky I was to have a total stranger take me on a tour. We visited some amazing cheese shops, flower markets, and souvenir shops. We took several photos and even had lunch together, as if we were old friends. I was able to make a few great memories with a stranger, and I continue to enjoy those special moments through my photographs. Thanks to social networking sites, we have even remained friends online. This may seem like a unique experience to you. However, you would be surprised how often locals and other tourists will be happy to help you or even spend half a day showing you around. If you find yourself alone and shy in a new town, don't hesitate to introduce yourself to the locals and ask them to recommend places to eat or landmarks to see.

If you've been dreaming of traveling somewhere, set a date and start planning to make it happen. Remember to think positively about how your trip will turn out. Traveling is a great way to break out of your shyness because it gives you an excuse to approach people without seeming awkward or desperate. If you are a tourist, it's expected that you will stop people and ask for directions and suggestions. This is a great opportunity to practice engaging in conversation. Remember: it's a small world after all. There is no need to be afraid of the people you'll meet or the amazing things you'll see when you travel, whether you're with a companion or alone.

99.

Visualization Helps Heal Shyness

While watching some pregame get-you-in-the-mood programming on TV, I saw a segment in which a number of athletes talked about how they would visualize the game before it started, imagining how well they would perform. Though I first studied the practice decades ago, I don't think I've ever heard it discussed so casually. Visualization has now become the norm for those wishing to excel in almost any area of life. It can help you make your life better and eliminate your shyness.

The practice of clinical guided imagery, or visualization, has been used in various ways. For many years, therapists have been focusing on its use in helping people heal their physical bodies and their emotional states. Numerous research studies have shown how beneficial this practice can be. Visualization is not meant to take the place of traditional medical interventions, but it can definitely enhance them. It is also a great tool for relaxation, which can be very challenging for anyone who deals with shyness or is going through physical or emotional distress.

Exercise

Sit in a comfortable position in a quiet place. Let out your breath until your lungs feel empty. Begin inhaling through your nose, first filling your stomach, then the bottom section of your lungs, followed by the middle, and, finally, the top of your lungs. Hold that for a count of five. Slowly exhale through your mouth. Feel your body relaxing, releasing all tension as you exhale. Let all worries fall away from your mind and let go of any distress in your body. Do three cycles of this deep breathing.

In this relaxed state, see in your mind's eye what it is that you want for your life. Then begin with one small element of that desire and embellish it. What else would you add to your vision? What would make it more tangible to you? Be as specific as possible. You may want to visualize yourself being more outgoing and enjoying yourself around people you don't know yet. This is how you begin healing the condition. If you are giving a speech, imagine it going perfectly, hearing the audience (or your boss) say "Wow, he/

she's great,'' and see yourself doing well and enjoying the process.

Every fellow therapist with whom I've spoken agrees
that positive guided imagery can be an effective practice in
overcoming shyness. There are also CDs, DVDs, and soft-
ware applications available to help you. If you have a hard
time coming up with images in your head, viewing a screen
can assist you. Modern technology has given us some great
tools to heal ourselves.

One thing that encourages athletes and shy folks alike is
feeling victorious. Actually feeling the positive emotions of
winning the game or healing your shyness may give you that
extra energy you need. Whether experiencing the pleasure
of winning a game or feeling the positive emotions associated with triumphing over your shyness, these visualization
techniques can provide you with that extra energy to take
charge of your body and your mind.

100.

When You Need to
Make an Apology

For someone who is shy, having to make an apology, especially a public one (such as at work) can be an agonizing

ordeal—so much so that I have known people to resign rather than fess up and say they were sorry. Not saying you are sorry when it is appropriate and obvious can derail an otherwise healthy relationship.

Whenever anyone asks me how I became successful, I always give the same answer: I've made a lot of mistakes and I've learned from them. So can you. Not being able to say you are sorry out of embarrassment, another type of shyness, is just not good form. I know it's hard to admit to your kid or your spouse or your boss that you were wrong, but it's better than everyone walking around with hurt feelings forever.

When you apologize, show that you mean it deeply. In order to forgive you, the person you hurt needs to be able to know that you feel his or her pain. Once you understand this, and if you repeat back what you heard someone say, the person you hurt will feel that you are making the heartfelt apology that is needed to create closure and help you both move on. Ask if there is anything you can do to make up for what happened. By offering just compensation, you are giving more than just words; you are offering to give of yourself, and that will go a long way. In most cases, nothing will be asked of you, but when it is, you must follow through in a way that works for both of you. It may mean doing the dishes or taking on someone else's work, but it really will help you heal the rift and give you more strength. Yes, this action of apology will help you reduce your shyness factor.

Admitting when you are wrong is a very adult thing to do. Even when you've wronged someone, naming the wrong and offering a targeted, specific apology will help boost your self-esteem. Yes, it's stressful, but it's the kind of stress makes you better at running the human race.

BONUS TIP
Writing Your Way Through Shyness

Journaling has always been a tried and true way of tuning into your feelings and helping yourself make changes you desire. It's a very simple process, and one that can be done totally on your own, but it's surprising how few people take advantage of this wonderful healing process.

There are tons of types of journals available, perhaps as many as there are people writing in them, and it is totally okay for you to have your own style and way of using this healing technique to make your life a better place to be. Some people choose to write every day. Author Julia Cameron, who wrote *The Artist's Way*, recommends something she calls "morning pages," in which you write longhand every morning. This isn't going to work for everyone, and truth be told, I think she meant this to be mostly helpful to writers, but we all can benefit from the exercise. Just as some people take morning runs while others prefer to walk in the evening, there are numerous ways to approach journaling. If writing daily is helpful to you, give yourself the tools and every opportunity to allow it to happen. I have given up other important things to write instead; it is a priority for me, and not just as a profession. I find it emotionally calming.

Another journaling technique that is less intense is called the gratitude journal. The process is quite simple:

every night, before you go to bed, you write down three to five things that you are grateful for. The trick is that you can't reuse the same ones every day; you have to search your soul for what gives you gratitude and write it down. Because you do it before you sleep, the gratitude seeps into your subconscious, and within a couple of weeks many people feel more positive. It can do wonders for your shyness because it will make you feel more confident about yourself and your life. It will also allow you to bring in more positive feelings from those you care for. It allows you to share our feelings privately and then heals the thoughts that make you want to retreat from others, by gently changing the way you think about yourself and how you respond to situations that make you nervous.

Now go to the stationary store or your local bookstore and buy yourself a nice blank book that you can fill with your thoughts of gratitude. If you'd rather type it, that's fine too. The point here is to get those feelings of fear and the ones of gratitude down on paper. This helps release the fear and shyness from your personality while helping you feel the warmth you have coming to you. It will make you stronger and give you some insights into yourself and where you really want to be in life. Your shyness does not have to stop you anymore, as long as you write it out.

INDEX

ABOUT THE AUTHORS

Honored by several professional associations, **Barton Goldsmith, PhD,** is a multi-award-winning psychotherapist, a syndicated columnist, and a recognized keynote speaker.

Since 2002, Dr. Goldsmith's weekly column, *Emotional Fitness*, which is now syndicated by Tribune Media Agency, and has been featured in almost 1,000 publications including the *San Francisco Chronicle*, the *Chicago Sun-Times*, the *Detroit News*, and *Time* magazine, giving him a substantial readership. He has been interviewed on numerous TV/radio shows and for many publications; his expert advice is regularly featured in *Cosmopolitan* magazine; he is the top blogger for *Psychology Today*; and his *Emotional Fitness* blog has had more than 10 million views.

Dr. Goldsmith—"Dr. G," to his fans—has authored several books, including: *Emotional Fitness for Couples: 10 Minutes a Day to a Better Relationship* was published by New Harbinger on Valentine's Day 2006, and the sequel, *Emotional Fitness for Intimacy; Sweeten and Deepen Your Love in Just 10 Minutes a Day* released by New Harbinger in April 2009. Dr. Goldsmith also published *Emotional Fitness at Work—6 Strategic Steps to Success Using the Power of Emotion*, the third in the *Emotional Fitness* book series, which was released in September 2009 by Career Press, who also published *100 Ways to Boost Your Self-Confidence: Believe in Yourself and Others Will Too* in May of 2010. *The Happy Couple*, another New Harbinger publication, was released on December 1, 2013.

He has appeared on CNN, *Good Morning America*, *Fox & Friends*, CBS News, NBC News, *Beauty and the Geek*, *The Ricki Lake Show*, and *The Mancow Muller Show*. Dr. Barton also served as the national spokesperson for the Mars Candy/My M&M's Treasured Moments Challenge, and is currently the national spokesperson for the SunTender Pre-Marital Mentoring Program. Dr. G also hosted a weekly radio show on NPR affiliate KCLU, with nearly 90,000 listeners from Los Angeles to Santa Barbara.

He received recognition from the City of Los Angeles for his work with survivors of the 1994 earthquake. His *Emotional Fitness* column was the winner of the Clark Vincent Award for Writing from the California Association of Marriage and Family Therapists. In addition, Dr. G received the Peter Markin Merit Award from the American Association of Marriage and Family Therapists for his humanitarian efforts. He has also been named as the recipient of the Joseph A. Giannantoino II Award in recognition of his contributions as an Outstanding Educator in the field of Addiction Medicine, given by the California Association of Alcoholism and Drug Counselors, who also inducted him into The CAADAC Hall of Fame on October 1, 2011. Dr. Goldsmith was a National Merit Scholar and a Professor of Psychology at Ryokan College, Los Angeles.

Dr. Goldsmith connects with audiences worldwide with his energetic, uplifting, and fun communication style. Not a button-down shrink, Dr. G has a unique ability to inspire and entertain that leaves his readers, viewers, and listeners always wanting more. Dr. G began working as a writer when his career in professional basketball was cut short because he only grew to be five feet, six inches tall.

Marlena Hunter, M.A., a marriage and family therapist and a UC graduate with an MA degree in psychology, has gained several years of experience in a number of clinical settings, including private practice. In addition, Ms. Hunter is a TMS technician and contributes to blogs and articles for online magazines. Ms. Hunter studied psychoanalysis and received European credits and certification for training in Austria, Germany, and France. She is a member of the American Psychological Association and The California Association of Marriage and Family Therapists.